Sounds of Fire

Sound Wisdom
for Single Christians

Sounds of Fire

Sound Wisdom
for Single Christians

by Tiffany Buckner

Anointed Fire™ House Christian Publishing
www.anointedfirehouse.com

I dedicate this book to its true Author: YAHWEH.
You are holy, faithful, merciful and sovereign. May your
name be glorified in this book.

Note from the Author (Please Read)

Dear Reader,

Great day to you and thank you for purchasing *Sounds of Fire*. I wanted to write this note for several reasons—one of them being to thank you and tell you how much I appreciate you. You are truly a blessing and I pray that God blesses, keeps and prospers you all the more. Every time you purchase a book from me, you allow me to continue to share the gospel of Jesus Christ with the world at whole— for that, I am grateful.

The next reason I wanted to write this note is to clarify what this book is about. It is a compilation of my social media statuses. These are points of wisdom that God shared with and through me. With that being said, please note that God shares new wisdom through us everyday. Some people are legalistic and when they see wisdom being shared, the very first thing they say is, "Give me scriptural backing." This means that they believe that God stopped speaking after the Bible was written and published. God will never go against His Word, but His wisdom is infinite. This means that His wisdom is never-ending and each time He speaks, He confirms what He has already spoken. He is <u>not</u> stuck on repeat.

I know I don't have to say this to everyone, but I thought it was necessary to come out and explain to the *one percent* of people who think that God is either dead or mute that:

1. God still speaks through His prophets and His people. If He didn't, He wouldn't need prophets! Then again, some people don't believe that prophets still exist! They think that all of God's prophets are dead.
2. Prophets are not parakeets who cite pre-recorded scriptures again and again. We are mouthpieces for God to speak through and He shares new wisdom each and every time He speaks!
3. This book is a compilation of social media statuses. I don't know a soul who writes a status and then, shares a scripture to back up that status.

I know that I don't have to explain this to the majority of you, but when legalists come out and try to discredit what the Holy Spirit is saying through His people, they do a huge injustice to the body of Christ because of their limited, legalistic views. I normally don't address people like this, but because I intend to continue recording and resharing the wisdom God has shared with and through me, I wanted to address the topic of legalism. Legalism is being stuck, limited, religious and foolish! It means to have religion without the Holy Spirit. This is to ensure that anyone who is unintentionally legalistic can seek the heart of God for new understanding and for true salvation. This is also designed to serve notice to the devil that you will NOT shut me up! I will continue to share God's infinite wisdom and I won't close my heart to Him the moment I close my Bible!

To everyone else, thank you once again for your love and continued support. You are the reason that my books continue to receive five star reviews and attention. I appreciate you and thank God for you. This journey has been awesome—to say the least. I look forward to sharing with you more of what God is sharing with me. I love and appreciate you more than you know.

Do me a favor. Continue to share this wisdom via social media and offline as God leads you. It will surely bless someone else. When you share the statuses, be sure to mention which "Sound" it is; for example, (hashtag) SoundOfFire001. This way, people who have not heard about *Sounds of Fire* or its twin, *Proverbs of Fire* will know how to find and purchase this book.

Again, you are great, blessed and most definitely loved!

Your sister in Christ,
Tiffany

Table of Contents

Introduction

Fire releases several sounds, depending on what it comes in contact with. For example, when doused with water, fire often makes a sizzling sound. When it touches wood, it makes a crackling sound. When fire comes in contact with the wind, it makes a roaring sound. The point is that fire releases a sound when it comes in contact with something; this includes people.

Hebrews 12:29 refers to God as a "consuming fire." Why is this? First, you must consider the nature and power of fire. The three properties of fire are heat, fuel and air. All of these elements are needed to start a fire.

Heat represents righteousness (in our case). We cannot be lukewarm, but we must be either hot or cold. A believer who is hot is a believer who is active in the things of the Lord. A cold believer is a dead believer.

The Greek word for wind and spirit is "pneuma" and is often used to represent the Holy Spirit. When God breathed the breath of life into Adam, man became a living soul.

Fuel is representative of faith. When a righteous believer has faith in God, that believer provokes God (the consuming fire) to move in his or her situation. No mortal thing can stand against the power of fire because fire alters the state of whatsoever it touches, and so does God.

The truths in this book will consume many of the lies you've been told. The goal of this manuscript is to present random truths to you so that the state of your mind will be changed so much that your life will have no choice but to change as well.

Sounds of Fire is a collection of wisdom in the form of quotes, advice and anecdotes, mostly of which were shared on social media by Tiffany Buckner. This book ensures that these truths will not be buried on the Internet, but will instead be gathered together so that they can continue to help believers from all around the world.

Sounds of Fire

Chapter 1

Sound of Fire 001
If you're asking God for a husband more than you're asking Him for wisdom, knowledge and understanding, you are asking to become a foolish wife!

Sound of Fire 002
A seductress is nothing but a beautifully decorated graveyard where foolish men go to die.

Sound of Fire 003
It is possible to be soul-tied to several people while you're legally married to one person. That's why many marriages end; one or both of the spouses weren't truly free to marry.

Sound of Fire 004
Every night before I go to bed, I take out the trash even though, in most cases, it is not full. Why do I do this? Because I do not want roaches or any other insects to come forging for food in my house at night. If you leave food lying around, something is bound to come looking for it. Why don't we understand this about unforgiveness?
Unforgiveness is demon food.
God told us to not let the sun set on our wrath, or give place to the devil.
Did you know that when you go to bed angry at someone, you provide demons with a key to your heart? You are allowing demons to move in for the sake of being mad at somebody. That's why you need to take out the trash before you go to bed!

Forgive folks as soon as they offend you. If you have trouble doing it, go before God and ask Him for an extra dose of humility.

If you have to repeatedly forgive someone (except the spouse or children), you may want to pray about your relationship with that person.

It's a whole new day. Don't bring yesterday into today.

Remember, Satan goes about seeking whom he may devour. Don't let an unforgiving heart turn you into demon food.

Sound of Fire 005
Some people are snakes. Some people are snake charmers.

Sound of Fire 006
Some people are storms. Some people are storm chasers.

Sound of Fire 007
Refusing to read the Bible does not make you exempt from it!

Sound of Fire 008
Love will never require you to be a doormat! Know the difference between love and tolerance.

Sound of Fire 009
Loving yourself makes you reject any and everyone who doesn't have the capacity to love you.

Sound of Fire 010

Some of y'all be praying for God to hold your tongue and to help you to close your mouth, but the right prayer is to ask Him to change your heart. Out of the abundance of the heart, the mouth speaks!

Sound of Fire 011

Sometimes, we aren't being attacked by the same devil; we're just retaking a test because we failed it the first time!

Sound of Fire 012

Never want something for someone more than that person wants it for himself or herself.

Sound of Fire 013

The imagination arena of the mind is the waiting room of the heart.

Whatever you don't cast down ultimately has to be cast out because it will leave the waiting room of your mind and make its way into your heart. From there, it becomes a belief. A belief is information received in the heart as true. Sometimes, thoughts that weren't cast down aren't easily received into our hearts and this is when we wrestle with double-mindedness.

Double-mindedness comes when two or more beliefs are waging war against each other, because both beliefs were allowed to sit in the "waiting room" too long, or the person allowed both beliefs in, hoping to test them later. This always brings confusion, doubt, restlessness and worry ... all of which are demonic. Beliefs are what drives our choices, perceptions, perspectives and ultimately, what we receive in life. That's why God said to guard your heart (belief system), for out of it pours the issues of life. Do not give every thought a free pass into your heart. Test the spirit that brings the thought and do not forget to pray. It's time to clean up the waiting room. If the heart needs to be clean, it's time to find a Godly deliverance minister to help clean up the house. Let's not give place to the devil. We have to be intentional about our walk in Christ Jesus.

Sound of Fire 014

Anytime you follow a scripture up with the word "but," you have found your area of unbelief.

Sound of Fire 015

When you have a question to ask someone who is in the same house with you, the same building as you or anywhere within your ear's reach, you will shout out the question if the person isn't too close to you. But notice this ...the more important the question is to you, the closer you'll get to that person to get the answer. That's because the details do matter in situations that we label as important. Why aren't you taking that same approach with God? If something is important to you, you shouldn't offer up the same distant, religious prayers that you normally offer up before dinner. You need to draw closer to Him; you need to enter into His presence. He wants intimate communication with us, not distant requests begging Him to give us the desires of our hearts.

Sound of Fire 016

Sin will only reign in your life when you are still submitted to the belief that somewhere, somehow, you'll manage to extract a blessing from it. The truth is—sin extracts the blessings out of you.

Sound of Fire 017

You need new information if you want to see a transformation. Let me explain.

The word information is broken down to two words: in and formation. The word "formation" means to be arranged, aligned or placed in a certain order. This aligning is necessary for something to take place. In the Bible, many events had to occur before a prophecy was fulfilled. In life, two people most come together in order for a child to be born. Therefore, when you are receiving in-formation, you are being aligned to cause something to take place. This means that the information you receive isn't just mere words designed to "educate" you. Every word that enters your heart and mind is aligning you for something to take place. If you're out of the will of God, a group of events will align to bring forth the wages of sin: death. That's why we say things like, "If she hadn't gone over to _____ house, this wouldn't have happened." Nevertheless, whatever it was that happened was a part of a series of events—some of which should have never taken place. It all happened because of the information she had received. What's the conclusion here? We should be feasting on the Word of God; that way, we are taking in the right information that will bring us into alignment with God's will for our lives. Every choice you make is a result of the information you have received.

Sound of Fire 018
You will always attract what you are, so if you want to be blessed, start by being a blessing.

Sound of Fire 019
Ladies, it is not in a man's nature to respect what he didn't have to work for. Where do you think the term "easy" came from? Some women work tirelessly trying to make a man love them, but a wise woman gets and maintains his respect. When a man respects you, he will trust you with his heart and he will trust that he can safely love you. A man's love for you can never surpass his respect for you.

Sound of Fire 020
Many believers claim Jesus as their Lord and Savior but, in truth, they want Him to be their Savior but not their Lord. The word "Lord" means "Master." It is the one you serve; the one you submit to. Folks don't want to submit to the Master, but they want Him to reward them like they are His servants. That's like getting hired by Walmart, putting on a Walmart work vest, and then going to work for Target. After that, you expect Walmart to hand you a check at the end of the week just because you LOOKED like a Walmart employee while working for Target.

Sound of Fire 021

You can't bathe in a bucket of crap and then pray the flies away. Flies are drawn to waste. The same goes for sin. Demons are attracted to sin. You can't sit in sin and then pray the devils away. If you choose to sin against God, you are choosing to embrace the sins, the demons and the consequences of your sins. Don't be deceived. Flies are to waste as demons are to sin.

Sound of Fire 022

Fear is just misplaced faith.

Sound of Fire 023

True worship doesn't come from the mouth. It comes from the heart.

Sound of Fire 024

Who I was and who I am are not the same. If you are familiar with the old me, you will need a new heart and a new mind to receive the new me.

Sound of Fire 025

Let me pose a question to you. God looks at the heart of man. He knows that we can make our mouths say whatever we want them to say. For that reason, God deals with your heart because it is, in a sense, your little black box. It stores what you hear, talk about, read and believe. Because we know right from wrong, we allow ourselves to say the right things, even when we believe the wrong things. So, here's the question. If God was to turn off your will and make you run only off what you have stored in your heart within the last six months, would you still be able to call yourself Christian? Could you lead others to Christ with what pours out of you? Would unbelief, gossip, blasphemies and perverted speech come out of you, or would you sincerely have the heart of God? These questions are important because they challenge us to remove our religious masks and access our heart conditions.

Sound of Fire 026

I am in love with the Most High God and I'm not ashamed of it! I will shout it from the rooftops if necessary. YAHWEH is my everything!

Sound of Fire 027

Rebellion is as the sin of witchcraft.
Manipulation is witchcraft.
Reading your horoscope is believing in the powers of the devil and submitting to witchcraft.
(Ladies) Trying to take authority over your husband or pastor is witchcraft.
Using sex to "hook" someone or get them to love you is witchcraft.

Sound of Fire 028

Witchcraft doesn't always involve a pointed hat and long-nosed woman stirring a pot, or some woman wearing a turban and playing with a crystal ball. Witchcraft can be practiced by a man or a woman! Some of the worst witchcraft is the evil that goes unnoticed.

Anytime you submit to any form of witchcraft, you unknowingly invite in familiar spirits and submit to them. And guess what? They won't go away just because you're praying in tongues and running around the church (they'll just sit there and enjoy the ride). You will NEED to repent for the sin that allowed them in AND you will need to be delivered from them.

Sound of Fire 029

Would you feel at home if your spouse pointed to a room and said, "You can go in every room of this house except that one?" Guess what? God doesn't feel at home when you close off certain areas of your life and heart to Him, all the while begging Him to go into the off-limit areas and give you the tools to help you remain as rebellious as you are.

Sound of Fire 030

At any given moment, we are either vessels of God's love or vessels of pride. Whatever we choose to be determines the direction we head in and who we are making a delivery to.

Sound of Fire 031

Sex is not "making love" since love has existed before the foundation of the Earth. Sex is an expression FIRST of your love and fear of God or lack thereof, and then it is an expression of your relationship with the person you are engaging with. You see, if you love and fear the Lord, you won't engage in sex outside the covenant of marriage, but if you don't love or fear Him, you will submit to whatever or whomever it is that you do fear. Know this ... we all fear something, whether it's God or losing the people whom God did not connect us with. If you don't reverence God, you will not honor His love towards yourself or the person you have chosen to have sex with. Since you cannot "make love," you will engage in meaningless encounters that serve to satisfy your lusts and serve as a generic replacement for the love you have rejected, but in the end, how you feel about God and how you feel about yourself will carry over into your relations and your relationships.

Sound of Fire 032

You can receive healing and deliverance in your own home if you'll only dare to have an intimate relationship with God and press into His presence as often as you can.

Sound of Fire 033

One of the most powerful things you can say to God is, "I need you and I can't do this on my own. Please take over." I have seen instant turnarounds in my life many times by simply humbling myself and acknowledging that I am nothing but dirt.

Sound of Fire 034

Can I be honest and tell you that a lot of you aren't being "attacked" by the enemy; you're just having another fight with him? Here's the thing. If a person that I do not know was to walk up to me, take my car keys and drive off in my car, I could call the police and have him arrested. What he did was ILLEGAL. Because he has no rights to me, he had no rights to my keys. However, if I'm married to a man and he took my car keys and drove off in my car, by law, the car is his too! It is considered community property! So, to law enforcement, the two of us would just be having a fight and they would not get involved. Why? Because what he did was LEGAL! Community property laws dictate that all property (except inheritances and gifts) are joint property between the husband AND the wife! The ONLY way I could get my rights back to my car would be to divorce or annul that marriage. Guess what? It's the same principle with backslidden, unrepentant, rebellious believers! When the enemy takes their stuff, he's not "attacking" them; they are just having ANOTHER fight! What Satan takes, he has rights to; it's community property because sin gave him the LEGAL right to do so! That's why it is error to try to help a backslidden believer recover or hold on to their stuff! They need to repent and take away Satan's rights to their stuff! If you end up interceding for them to maintain the stuff without repentance, get ready ... they will be calling you A LOT because they will reconcile with Satan and it's only a matter of time before they have another fight!

Sound of Fire 035
Warfare 101: Just because you can't see it doesn't mean that it's not there.

Sound of Fire 036

Love will never send you to hell, so if your associations are leading you towards everlasting destruction, please know that they are not connected to you by love. They are on demonic assignment. Don't let them get a passing grade on that assignment.

Sound of Fire 037

Elevation is ALWAYS preceded by a renewed mind.

Sound of Fire 038

A storm can be made to serve you if you learn how to speak to it.

Sound of Fire 039

Oftentimes, we have to retake the tests of life (trials) because we keep trying to change the answers. God's Word will never and has never returned to Him void.

Sound of Fire 040

Stop settling for people who think they are settling for you!

Sound of Fire 041

During sex, there is always an impartation! If the sexual contact is between two people who are not legally married, the impartation will be demonic because sin gives demons the legal ground to come into and operate in your life. And demons don't play by your rules, nor are there any rules in warfare that command them to play nice or be merciful.

Understand this ... we are always submitting to something or somebody. Sex is a form of submission; it is submitting our bodies to whatever or whomever we've submitted our hearts to. The person or the thing (sex toy) you are submitting to will be the lord of your life. That's why we wait until marriage to physically submit ourselves to spouses who are in submission to God; that way, we fully submit to God and Satan has no rights to us, our marriages or our possessions! When an impartation is being made, it needs to be a godly one, otherwise whatever is imparted into you will begin to devour you!

Sound of Fire 042

The average believer looks for loopholes in the Word of God that would allow them to creatively disobey God, all the while remaining in His will. This place does NOT exist. Instead, what happens is—the believer begins to engage in self deception and without knowing it, he or she steps right outside of God's will and directly into the witchcraft of rebellion. From there, they become religious, presenting their works and words before God, all the while, their hearts are far from Him. They begin to count their deeds and constantly remind God of the many good things they've done. But, God's more focused on the current state of the saint versus their past or present deeds. This is how so many people who wear Christian tee-shirts and go to what's nothing more (to them) than a religious pep rally every Sunday, end up as prisoners of sin. They convince themselves that there is a right way to do wrong when there isn't.

Suddenly, their choices find and confront them, and that's when they call upon the name of the Lord for real. They stop chanting His name and they actually start calling it! Don't be that person! Don't be average. Average represents the natural, but peculiar represents the supernatural. Be peculiar. Let God lead you in all things; you have no choice but to trust Him—or you'll end up trusting Satan! There are no neutral grounds! Let's stop playing church and let's start actually being the church!

Sound of Fire 043

Understand this ... what the enemy is doing to this nation is sifting it! This war isn't against flesh and blood; it's against powers, principalities and the rulers of this dark world! The blind see colors, but those who have eyes to see will see what's behind the masks! Fight in the spirit because that's where the war is! Don't fight with the flesh because if you do, the enemy will take every ounce of uncrucified flesh that you have and use it against you!

Sound of Fire 044

Trials don't come to break you; they come to refine you and set you apart from the uncommitted.

Sound of Fire 045

A storm is oftentimes nothing more than you being chased out of your comfort zone.

Sound of Fire 046

Solomon built a temple for the Lord and it was beyond beautiful! He used some of the finest materials to build this temple. Even the floor was overlaid with gold! The temple was splendid. Nevertheless, God does not dwell in buildings made with man's hands; He dwells in us! We are the temples of the Holy Spirit! So, here's the question. How much of your heart is He allowed to dwell in? Can He have full roam of your heart or is He restricted to certain areas? Are there only certain days of the week that He's allowed to dwell in you (example: Sunday mornings) before He's handed yet another eviction notice? What does God's dwelling place in you look like? Is it a castle decorated with holiness, perfumed with praise and filled with the sounds of pure worship? Or is it a small dungeon filled with the stench of unforgiveness, decorated with the photos of every man or woman you have an ungodly soul-tie with? Is it infested with unclean spirits and filled with the agonizing sounds of you murmuring and complaining?

Ask yourself what type of dwelling place you are presenting to the Lord, and then clean it up! His dwelling place today should look far better than the one you gave Him yesterday. Now, that's true advancement in the Kingdom!

Sound of Fire 047

The more I die to self, the less weapons the enemy can find to use against me. Understand this: Satan's favorite weapon against you is YOU! When I died to me, those old dysfunctional emotions had no place to operate and I started looking for the wisdom in every storm rather than focusing on the storm itself!

Sound of Fire 048
It is possible to reject a blessing because you don't think you deserve it or you don't think it deserves you.

Sound of Fire 049
The safest place to be is in the will of God. Don't you dare go anywhere else.

Sound of Fire 050
If you want God to show up at your wedding, don't marry Satan.

Sound of Fire 051
When you embrace the surface of the Word, but not the depth of it, you miss understanding. This is where misunderstandings come from.

Sound of Fire 052
If you're still reading your horoscope while professing your faith in Jesus, you are double-minded and unstable in ALL your ways! You have opened a door for the enemy and he will use that opportunity to attack you at will. Close EVERY demonic access door in your life and stop dabbling with the occult!

Sound of Fire 053

You are beautifully and wonderfully made. You are a masterpiece because you were created by the Master Himself.

Sound of Fire 054

It's great to talk to God, but it's even better to hear back from Him. Listen for His response; don't just talk all over Him. The average person talks to God, but does not hear back from Him because they've mastered speaking, but they have not mastered listening.

Sound of Fire 055

Your value isn't determined by what others say or believe about you; it is determined by the One who created you. And to Him, you were worth dying for.

Sound of Fire 056

A woman who uses seduction to capture a man is a woman who had no wisdom to capture the attention of a man of God.

Sound of Fire 057

You can't choose your own way and invite God into a setting that He did not set up! You have to accept the invitation He has extended to you and that's when you'll see Him move for real!

Sound of Fire 058

Are you ready for the next chapter or are you still telling yesterday's story?

Sound of Fire 059

Guys, tell yourself this every day: My seed is too valuable to be deposited into the wrong bank.

Sound of Fire 060

Ladies, tell yourself this every morning: I am favor manifested.

Sound of Fire 061

Time spent with God is never time wasted.

Sound of Fire 062

A person should make several trips to the altar (salvation, deliverance) before you take them to the altar and marry them. If their first trip to the altar is to marry you, your next few trips to the altar will be for prayer, more prayer and eventually deliverance.

Sound of Fire 063

Prayer changes things, but an intimate relationship with God changes you.

Sound of Fire 064

Oftentimes, a manifestation is nothing but the light of God exposing an infestation of demonic spirits operating in a man or woman.

Sound of Fire 065

Yes, sex may make him stick around a little longer, just like sin gives demons the right to stick around. Submitting yourself to God and resisting the devil takes away Satan's legal grounds and causes him to flee. That means that by obeying God and refusing to be moved by the darts of the enemy (temptation, fear, unsound doctrine, pride, unforgiveness), you set yourself up for full-out deliverance, and that's a good thing! Why don't you understand this when it comes to an ungodly man? By not submitting to him and by not giving him the sin offering, you are choosing God over that man, so he has no choice but to flee, and that's a good thing! We should always celebrate being delivered from demons regardless of what form they come in.

Sound of Fire 066

If you don't have an active, consistent prayer life, you have become active prey for the enemy and he will consistently attack you.

Sound of Fire 067

The heart is like a sponge. It soaks up whatever you subject it to or submerge it in. That's why people who watch reality TV dance violently around the church with no regard for their neighbors. That violent spirit starts manifesting itself—even in their dancing. They bang tambourines, barely missing their neighbors and oftentimes bump, hit and fall all over their neighbors because they need deliverance! Don't allow something into your eyes and ears that you do not want to pour out of your life.

Sound of Fire 068

If you have to lead him in purity, you will have to lead him away from impurity. Marriages like that become nothing but a power struggle between a lost husband and the woman who thought she could save him.

Sound of Fire 069

A man "desires" his wife, but a perverted man lusts after his girlfriend. Lust is nothing but desire that's out of order and out of control.

Sound of Fire 070

Never allow loneliness to lead you into the company of the wrong people.

Sound of Fire 071

People who attempt to read the Bible without the help of the Holy Spirit oftentimes become legalistic conspiracy theorists with big mouths, a readiness to speak and no real power to speak of. Ask God to give you understanding of His Word; that way, you don't become a religious promoter of self and biblically inspired false doctrine.

Sound of Fire 072

When you sincerely love the Lord, everywhere you go is your

prayer room.

Sound of Fire 073

God uses the natural to explain that which is spiritual because we understand natural things. I want you to imagine this: It's Sunday morning and you're still at home about to head out to church. Right before you leave, there is a knock at the door. It's Satan. He's not covered in red skin, nor does he have a pitchfork or a pointy tail, but he's still Satan nonetheless. You tell him to make himself at home. You tell him that you're about to head out to church, but before leaving, you show him the vault, give him the password to that vault, give him your bank account information, show him where your kids are (who, by the way, now see him as family) and tell him every secret you have. After that, you head out to church. While there, you whoop and holler and before the night is over, your feet are swollen from all the dancing you've done and you're passed out (but conscious) halfway between the altar and the front row of the pews. The ushers have come and covered you up and you get up feeling like you've done your due diligence to God. After church, you head on home to check on Satan. Surely, after such a powerful church service, he can't still be in your home—or if he's still there, that mean footloose you did must have made it impossible for him to misbehave. Somehow, you think he's at your house baking cookies, watering the garden and reading bedtime stories to the kids. Obviously, you didn't know who he actually was and what he stood for! Understand this: If you open the door to Satan, you give him RIGHTS! You can do cartwheels around the church, drench your neighbor's favorite shirt with your tears and give the biggest offering, but if your heart is not submitted to God, sin is crouching at your door, waiting to take you out! Stop thinking that your works will justify you! Stop thinking that you can pay for the wages of your sin with religious performances. To cast Satan out, you must first close the door and disallow him from entering your life! Next, to keep him out, you need to operate in holiness because without holiness, no man will see God ... but they will see Satan. Stop doing works in the church trying to manipulate God and realize that you are the church and let Him work on you!

Sound of Fire 074

The day you try to save a man (romantically speaking) is the day you will need saving.

Sound of Fire 075

Satan goes about seeking whom he may devour. That means he cannot devour everyone! Who can he devour then? The Bible tells us that if we submit ourselves to God and resist the devil, he will flee from us. This means that he cannot devour a believer who is in submission to God! Nevertheless, a saint who dabbles with darkness is definitely on his menu! Submitting with your mouth is not the same as submitting that heart of yours! When Satan sees believers who don't fully believe the Word, he starts to appeal to their lustful states, drawing them further and further away from God by the hem of their lusts until he thinks he's gotten them to a place where he can successfully devour them without any interference (true intercession) from the submitted saints. You see, when a believer doesn't fully submit, that believer will begin to distance himself or herself from truly submitted saints because darkness hates light! That's when you hear people start saying things like, "They're so heavenly minded that they are no earthly good" or "It don't take all that!" That believer will surround himself or herself with religious parakeets (people who've remembered scriptures, religious movements and the like; people who've learned to mimic what they've seen and heard ... people who have a form of Godliness, but deny the power thereof). Such people lack the faith needed to successfully intercede for others. Those are the churches where there are more people on the sick and shut-in list than there are in the congregation. Let's submit saints! Let's press all the way in until we begin to look more like Him, sound more like Him and be more like Him.

Sound of Fire 076
The lessons in life are inevitable. Either we learn them or we become them.

Sound of Fire 077
We often marry a person's potential, but end up divorcing that person's reality.

Sound of Fire 078
No weapon formed against God's people will prosper; we

know this, but what happens when you form weapons against yourself with your words and choices? It's simple: You keep yourself from prospering!

Sound of Fire 079

People will always teach you what they've mastered or what's mastered them! A stock broker will teach you the ins and outs of the stock market, a dancer will teach you how to move your body and a prisoner will show you the way around the prison he or she is in. An overcomer will teach you how to overcome, but a defeated soul will teach you how to adapt to defeat! People will always lead you to their master!

Sound of Fire 080

In the Bible, you'll notice that there were several references to what a person said in their heart as opposed to what they said out loud. For example, Psalms 14:1 reads "A fool says in his heart that there is no God." Or when Abraham laughed in his heart at the idea of being a father at his age (Genesis 17:17). This means that our hearts are having a conversation with God long before we can even open our mouths. That's why it's dangerous to think that you can say one thing in your heart and then, lift something entirely different up to the Lord in prayer.
He knows your heart.
It is better to be truthful with Him than to say what you think He wants to hear because by doing so, you are attempting to deceive the all-knowing, ever-living, Almighty God.

Be honest with Him.
Honesty is the prelude to true deliverance.

Sound of Fire 081
Sometimes, your ticket to freedom is wrapped up in the hands of someone you don't like. God does this so that you can humble yourself to get set free!

Sound of Fire 082
Debt is the direct result of impatience.

Sound of Fire 083
When should you sow seeds in a person? It's simple. Look at their fruit! If they are a garden of blessings and favor, they are obviously good ground because God is sowing into them, but if they are graveyards where money goes to die, anything you give them will end up with a headstone. Of course, when dealing with the poor—their situations being the result of conditions that are out of their control as opposed to a result of their poor choices—anytime you give to them, you are lending to the Lord and He will pay you back. If you give to people who are in bondage because of their choices (if they have not repented), God is not obligated to pay you back; instead, you will reap from the spirit in which you've sown into.

Sound of Fire 084
You are either the lender or you're the borrower. You can't be both.

Sound of Fire 085

When you are backslidden, you don't ask for favor; you ask for mercy.

Sound of Fire 086

Righteousness was designed to scare the devil away, but sin invites him in. That's why most folks end up marrying the weapons that were formed against them.

Sound of Fire 087

One of Satan's greatest deceptions is convincing folks that God is blind.

Sound of Fire 088

You can't enter holy matrimony doing unholy things.

Sound of Fire 089

There is a difference between wasting your time versus investing it.

Sound of Fire 090

At any given moment, you are on assignment. The question of the hour is ... who sent you?

Sound of Fire 091

You can't wait for your God-appointed spouse while entertaining somebody else's.

Sound of Fire 092

Obedience precedes elevation.

Sound of Fire 093

To a man who has faith, a storm is but a gust of wind. To a man who has no faith, a gust of wind is a storm.

Sound of Fire 094

There is a womb that's pregnant by you right now—but whose womb is it? Did you impregnate sin with your unrepentant, rebellious ways or is Heaven getting ready to give birth on your behalf? Life and death are in the power of the tongue; what exactly have you released? What you've released is what you can expect! Did you know that speaking blessings followed by word curses is pretty much the same as releasing a seed and then aborting it? What exactly is about to be born to you? If you impregnated rebellion, you need to repent (turn all the way away from your sins) and uproot that seed before rebellion gives birth! Rebellion has some UGLY children and you do NOT want to parent one of them!

Sound of Fire 095

God yearns to hear from you.

Sound of Fire 096

Love and submission are a team. You can't have one without the other.

Sound of Fire 097
Faith and peace are a team. You can't have one without the other.

Sound of Fire 098
Content people are not contentious.

Sound of Fire 099
Stop trying to replace Jesus. He is irreplaceable.

Sound of Fire 100
I'm in love with Obedience. He is far better to me than my ex: Sacrifice.

Chapter 2

Sound of Fire 101
Every setback is nothing but a setup in the making.

Sound of Fire 102
Manipulation is witchcraft in infant form.
Anger is witchcraft as a toddler.
Wrath is witchcraft in its youth.
Rebellion is witchcraft as a teenager.
Bitterness is witchcraft as a young adult.
Word curses, slander, black magic, sorcery and the like are
witchcraft all grown up.

Sound of Fire 103
The you that you want to be will always wage war against
the you that you were designed to be. Don't kill your future
by trying to recreate yourself. God created you, so there's no
way for you to do better than Him and upgrade yourself. Any
changes you make to yourself outside of Him are
downgrades.

Sound of Fire 104
Holiness repels demons.

Sound of Fire 105
The Book of Revelations is the explanation of the beginning
and a revealing of a new beginning. Everything starts with
Alpha (God) and ends with Omega (God). Understand this.
Life is similar. Our greatest breakthroughs come only after a
great revelation. This revelation is an explanation of what

we've just come out of and a revealing of where we're going.

Sound of Fire 106
Woman of God,
You are favor manifested.

Sound of Fire 107
To the men ...
God said that he who finds a wife finds a good thing and obtains favor from the Lord. Understand that there is a difference between a woman and a wife.
A wife has already been declared a wife by God, but a woman is incomplete. She is not ready to take on the responsibilities of a wife, even though she's eager to enjoy the benefits. That's why she'll be so argumentative. So if you marry a woman, she will not become a wife; she will become a married woman. This means that you will not get favor from God; instead, you'll get the opposite of favor. I looked up the opposite of favor and according to thesaurus.com, it is:
disdain, disrespect, hindrance, hurt, injury, loss, opposition, stop, criticism, denial, denunciation, disadvantage, disapproval, dislike, disregard, fairness, hate, ill will, impartiality, meanness, and veto.
Sound familiar?

Sound of Fire 108
To the men ...
Beware of women who offer themselves up to you

physically, whether they do it directly or indirectly. Some women simply want to plant a seed in your mind so that it can produce fruit in your imaginations. Understand this. A woman who is free with her body is not free in the soulish realm, which means that there are other men soul-tied to her, plus, there are demonic spirits operating within her. That's why she's so free and open ... what's in her is trying to get to you. If you tangle yourself up with her, you give her and everything that's on the inside of her access to you. A woman after God's own heart understands her worth and will not offer herself up to you without you first sharing your last name with her. Why is this? She is favor manifested. She has more to offer than SEX! She will bring you PEACE and JOY all the days of your life, but if you get tangled up with a Delilah, she will expose you to the enemy.

Sound of Fire 109

Unforgiveness is unresolved debt. It is simply saying that the person you're mad at owes you something ... maybe it's an apology, money or a conversation. Either way, the issue is unresolved, meaning that even if you're no longer communicating with that person, you still have a relationship with them. But that doesn't mean they have a relationship with you! For some people, an apology won't suffice because they've added interest to the debt and they want to see blood. They want the people they are offended with to suffer and this is the evidence of a wicked, demon infested heart. They've let the sun set on their wrath many times, and now they have the same heart towards their enemies that Satan has. That's how unforgiveness works! It makes folks think and behave like Satan! God is love, so when we choose to love and forgive people, it makes us think and behave like God!

Life is all about resolve. You resolve it in your heart to forgive people; you release them, and move forward. In doing this, you turn over the debt to the debt collector (God). If they ask Him for forgiveness, He is willing to forgive them for their debts as long as they repent and are willing to forgive others for their debt. The same goes for you. That's the circle of love. Love never stops giving or forgiving.

Sound of Fire 110
Who God proves, He approves.

Sound of Fire 111
Everything has a sound and a feel to it. In the morning, we hear birds singing and we can feel the fresh morning breeze. When the evening comes, we hear crickets, cicadas and frogs. Just like the morning, the evening often has a distinct feel to it as well. As the evening wears on, the weather almost always gets cooler.

The same goes for our own personal seasons. There's a distinctive sound to every season and if you'll learn to tune in to it, you will not be overwhelmed with the weather that accompanies each season. For example, there are seasons when we hear God a lot, and then there are seasons when He doesn't seem to be saying much, but He's still talking. He just wants to teach you to hear His voice through what you see and feel! Think about the winter. No one has to tell us that it's winter time because we can feel the cold air and see the snow (whenever it does snow). God doesn't have to verbally tell us that it's winter; we have experienced winter before so we know what seasons we're in naturally! Sure, we've mastered the seasons of the Earth, but it's time for us to master the seasons of our lives. Life is so much easier when you know which season you're in.

Sound of Fire 112

A loveless marriage is the evidence that neither the husband nor the wife loved themselves or understood the love of God before they got married. You will always attract your own reflection.

Sound of Fire 113

Our marriage tradition is ... our fathers will walk us down the aisle (ladies) and hand us over to the men we're about to marry. This tradition is reminiscent of an old tradition where a man (or his father) had to ask the bride's father for her hand in marriage. The woman would then be betrothed to the man until the appointed day. Her father had to give the man permission to marry the woman, otherwise it was illegal for that man to touch that woman. God speaks to us through natural things and what He is demonstrating is that your covering should hand you to your next covering. The father covered, provided for and protected his daughter in the Old Testament days. When he gave her away, her new husband covered, provided for and protected his wife. This is what our Father is doing for us these days. He is the One who has the LEGAL right to give us away and when He hands us over to our spouses, it will be because He approved them AND they are covered by Him. This means that they will be able to effectively cover us. If you go and choose the wrong man, God will not give you to him; you will attempt to give yourself away and your relationship will be ILLEGAL ... Here's the problem in this...

... you don't belong to yourself so you can't LEGALLY give yourself away ...

So here's what will happen if you try.

You'll marry the guy hoping that he can help you find yourself ... you'll marry the guy hoping that he'll be able to make you happy. He can't.

God has the whole you hidden in Him and to "find yourself," you must search His heart and learn His ways.

Even if you find yourself, the man you chose won't know the hidden things regarding you. You can shout it at him, write it on paper and record a CD for him, but he won't be able to hear you. Why is this? Because only God can reveal His secrets. You are favor manifested, but the secret of your favor will only be revealed to the man God hands you to. That man will be able to meet God at the altar, take your hand and cover you because he is in agreement with God and God is in agreement with him. This means that God will cover him and God will cover you through him.

Sound of Fire 114

It is possible to chase the voice of God, but not the heart of

God.

Sound of Fire 115

Ladies, let God show you how you're supposed to be treated. If you don't fully surrender to Him, you won't experience Him as a deliverer, provider and keeper; which means you'll sell out to the first dude who offers you a better experience than your Christian experience. Surrender to God with your body, mind and spirit and once He demonstrates who He is (God is Love), you won't be so flattered when someone lusts after you because you will have experienced true Love ... and nothing can compare to that!

Sound of Fire 116

Life is not like a math problem. One plus one doesn't always equal two. If a person is soul-tied to other folks, one plus one may equal twenty six.

Sound of Fire 117

When you walk away from people, you aren't saying that you're mad at them; sometimes, you're simply saying that you have forgiven yourself.

Sound of Fire 118

Who you connect to is a direct reflection of what you think of yourself.

Sound of Fire 119

When a man attempts to lie with you before marriage, he is

calling you a whore. Just like we understand what the middle finger means when someone points it at us, we must understand what a man trying to uncover us (sex) before covering us (marriage) means. It is sign language and it translates as, "I have no respect for you or your God. If you want to keep me around, you must demonstrate the same dishonor and disrespect towards God that I am demonstrating to you now. You are unworthy of a wife title; you are but a whore to me. Now, what type of music do you want to listen to while I disrespect you in the name of love?"

Sound of Fire 120

Jesus Christ made the ultimate investment in us and said that our reasonable service to Him, meaning the least we can do, is to present our bodies as a living sacrifice to Him ... HOLY and ACCEPTABLE. What does this mean? It is possible to be abstinent and unholy.

Sound of Fire 121

The measure of love in a man is equivalent to the measure of the Word that man has in him.

Sound of Fire 122

When you take God for granted, you will end up in relationships with people who take you for granted. Why is that? Because sometimes, we deafen ourselves to the truth and when this happens, God has to speak to us through a hearing aid called "experience."

Sound of Fire 123

God is holy. This means that true love is holy. Anything else is just lust.

Sound of Fire 124

Breakthrough happens when you surrender wholeheartedly to God. Think about when a criminal surrenders to the authorities. He walks into the police station and turns himself in. He acknowledges his crimes and decides to face the consequences. He does this so he can do his time and finally embrace true freedom; after all, being free in body, while living in a state of fear is not freedom. It's having the appearance of freedom, but not the reality of it. I've learned that this is similar to surrendering to God. We go before the Lord, acknowledge our sins, repent of our sins and we have to face many of the problems that our sins produced if we want to embrace true freedom. Nevertheless, when facing these problems, we stop blaming folks and the devil and we press pass the critics so we can finally get to that place that God has ordained us to walk into. The moment God sets you free is the day of breakthrough. Breakthrough never stops because there is always an area that you need to be set free in, but like before, you go before God, acknowledge that error and prepare for God to give you the directions to get out of it. You press your way on through until you encounter breakthrough again. From there, the process restarts itself, but eventually you'll notice how much freer you are and how much happier you are. Press!

Sound of Fire 125
We never stop making mistakes.
We just have to stop making excuses.

Sound of Fire 126
Our knowledge and understanding are limited, but God's wisdom is without ends. Do not lean on your own understanding or operate from the limitations of your wisdom; lean on God so that you can go beyond your abilities and tap into God's supernatural abilities.

Sound of Fire 127
The whole armor of God will protect you from weapons that you didn't even know had been formed against you!

Sound of Fire 128
It's great to have experienced Christianity, but it is better to have experienced Christ.

Sound of Fire 129
You matter to God.

Sound of Fire 130
In every season's end, you will experience a lot of opposition designed to keep you from going to the next season. But you must remember, opposition is the opposing of your position in Christ or your position in sin. Satan opposes your position in Christ and Christ opposes your position in sin. If Christ isn't opposing you, sin has no right to you, and therefore,

whatever is opposing you is demonic.

Sound of Fire 131

Ministers, we can put our names on the front of a building and call it a church, but since we are the church, we need to make sure that God has His sign on the front door of our hearts.

Sound of Fire 132

In every new season, we are setting the stage for the next season. What are you doing and saying in this season? Believe it or not, it's releasing things into your life, so be sure to do, say and think the right things. Tomorrow, you'll be glad you did.

Sound of Fire 133

Forgiveness is focusing ahead because you believe that yesterday is nothing but an indication of what God has in store for you tomorrow. Unforgiveness is looking back because you believe that yesterday has the power to ruin your tomorrow.

Sound of Fire 134

Study and show yourself approved. No studying equals no approval!

Sound of Fire 135

Love never fails and hatred never wins. Remember that.

Sound of Fire 136

My life isn't a reflection of my works; it's a reflection of my repentance.

Sound of Fire 137

Dear woman of God,
For one man, you are nothing but a test.
For another man, you are a testimony.
Don't become one man's problem when God has created you to be another man's favor.

Sound of Fire 138

Our lives respond to our choices. I've learned that our thoughts, words and choices speak for us, and then, the Word of God responds to them all. From there, we see a manifestation of our realities, and these realities are a reflection of the dialogues that our lives are having with God.

Sound of Fire 139

When you open your mouth to identify yourself by a zodiac sign, in that very minute, you fall subject to the demons presiding over that sign. Demons have personalities, so you will pick up devils and notice how similar your personality is to others who are subject to that same demon. What you're identifying is a demonic personality that you have embraced as your own. Don't believe me? Walk into an authentic deliverance ministry and go to the front for prayer and watch them jokers manifest!

Sound of Fire 140

Never treat God like serving or obeying Him is a task. Would you want your spouse to treat intimacy with you like a task? Then don't do it to God.

Sound of Fire 141

God loves you better than you can possibly love yourself. That's why it makes no sense to be self-seeking. When you put self above God, you are robbing yourself of genuine, authentic love and replacing it with love that's been tainted by the cares of this world. You will then offer yourself to people who, like you, don't know or understand genuine love and they'll give you less than you are giving yourself. This is because you set your standards low when you put yourself above God. I love me, but God loves me more, so I trust Him to take care of me far more than I trust myself. He has never let me down, but I've let myself down many times. God above self. He won't have it any other way.

Sound of Fire 142

Satan is wicked; we know this, but he can really put together a cast. Think about some of your favorite shows. The producers were able to put together a cast of people that seem to fit so well together that we could not imagine them outside of the roles that they were cast in. Nobody could've imagined Heathcliff Huxtable without Clair (The Cosby Show), Michael without Jay (My Wife and Kids), Zack without Kelly (Saved by the Bell), Ricky without Lucy (the Lucy Show) or George without Louise (the Jeffersons). Nevertheless, when the credits cued, the actors and actresses went home to their real families. It was just an entertaining show that helped us to escape our realities and live vicariously through the actors or actresses if but for thirty minutes. Understand this ... Satan puts together casts too and he causes the greatest part of those relationships to play out in our minds. That's why there are so many soul-tied folks walking around who had to deal with the fact that it was all a show. At some point, the show was canceled and their lovers went back home. Don't exchange your reality for a bunch of fruitless fantasies. Let God write your love story; that way, it won't be just a show. When God has the pen, the credits cue every day when your spouse comes home to YOU!

Sound of Fire 143

You can't be who people want you to be and who God called you to be at the same time. Choose one.

Sound of Fire 144

You can't be that man's sex toy and God's prophetess. Once you submit yourself to that man in sexual immorality, you are rebelling against God; the bible tells us that rebellion is the same as the sin of witchcraft. For this reason, a fornicating prophetess cannot be trusted.

Sound of Fire 145

When the kingdom of darkness tells you to shut your mouth, it's because what you have to say is setting people free from it. When the kingdom of darkness tells you to keep on talking, it's because what you have to say is sending people to it.

Sound of Fire 146

You're not relevant until you become an issue. Google's first definition of the word "issue" is: *an important topic or problem for debate or discussion.* Understand this ... until hell comes together and discusses your downfall, you haven't even stood up yet.

Sound of Fire 147

Why do we shower or bathe daily? The answer is simple. So we won't bring yesterday's dirt and contaminants into today with us. We want to start the day afresh.
God tells us to do the same things with our hearts. He said to not let the sun set on your wrath. That means you should never go to bed with offense, malice or anger in your heart. You should resolve each issue within your heart, make peace with it, and then go to bed. That way, you don't bring yesterday's dirt (problems) and contaminants (problematic people and mindsets) with you into today.

Sound of Fire 148

I will never call another human being my everything or my rock. Those positions are taken.

Sound of Fire 149

It doesn't matter what position you pray in physically if your heart is not in submission to God.

Sound of Fire 150

The more honest I am with God, the more honest I've learned to be with myself.
The more honest I am with myself, the more honest I've learned to be with God.

Sound of Fire 151

The reason unforgiveness is so offensive to God, besides the fact that His Son died for our sins is ... we lose the power and potency of the lesson. You see, everything we do in love with godly intentions is a good seed, even if we sow it in the wrong people. Sometimes, we sow seeds and God intends to use those seeds sown to not only bless us but to bless and help the people we've sown them into. Nevertheless, we get so caught up in what we think we lost or wasted that we fail to see God's intentions. So we murmur, complain and slander folks, hoping to at least repair the damage done to our newly bruised egos. This essentially corrupts the seeds we've sown and disallows God from giving us a Godly harvest. This also keeps the people we are offended with from getting the lesson and promotion that the seed produces. In other words, we cause our good deeds to be evil spoken of.

Forgive, love and move forward. If you've sown godly seeds in people who didn't know the value of them, you have done the work of the Lord. Just don't keep sowing into them and don't abort the blessing by complaining or talking about them. In due season, you will reap if you do not faint (give up). Remember, God loves a cheerful giver!

Sound of Fire 152

Wherever we go in life, we must be wearing the proper clothing. You can't wear your pajamas in church, nor can you enter a five star restaurant wearing jeans. You must be clothed in the proper attire to enter the places that you want to enter.

The same goes for promotion.

Our mindsets are like garments. They will determine where we go and where we're not allowed. God is always changing our minds so that He can take us to greater places in Him. If you submit to the change, you will see swift promotion. If you reject the change, you will be held back.

Listen up saints. Satan is ALWAYS trying to get us to return to old mindsets. He promises that this time, things will be different. He says that you simply did things wrong the last time—but this is a LIE! It was your mindset that held you back, so it doesn't matter how well you disobey God or how loud you shout in the congregation; if you are not wearing the proper mindset, you will keep getting the same results! At the same time —if you went to a five star restaurant and you were dressed properly, but were accompanied by a person (relative or friend) who was not dressed properly, both of you would be denied entry. So, it is important who you try to take with you. Some of you keep getting retained because your heart is right before God, and yet you keep trying to take folks into places that their mindsets won't let them enter.

Sound of Fire 153

The Master only creates masterpieces and no masterpiece is common. It's one of a kind.

Sound of Fire 154

Elijah was commanded by God to go and live near the brook of Cherith. This was during a severe drought. God sent ravens to feed Elijah and he drank from the brook, meaning God supplied all of his needs in the midst of a famine and a drought.

Know this. God will never leave nor forsake His own because we bear His name. Nevertheless, if God says to go and live near the brook, you need to understand that that's where your provision is! The brook He's sent you to is where He's commanded the ravens to feed you. If you go and live elsewhere, you will become subject to whatever is happening in the land (your place of dwelling). Obey God. He knows what He's doing.

Sound of Fire 155

Church shoes and fancy wigs won't get you into heaven.

Sound of Fire 156

There's a past tense version of us and a present tense version of us. Nevertheless, God is always present. Live in today. Yesterday has passed, today is now and tomorrow is waiting.

Sound of Fire 157

Sometimes, we are willing to hear what God has to say to us, but we get offended when He has something to say about us. The truth of the matter is—true love is not always flattering. Anytime we chase good prophecies, but are offended at the sound of a godly rebuke, we are rejecting a true relationship with the Lord. He's not going to always offer us cars, houses, promotions and spotlights. Sometimes, He offers us a mirror. Understand this. He does this because He loves us. He wants us to see what's keeping us from being promoted and what's keeping us from looking like Him. Nevertheless, when we turn away from that mirror, all the while asking Him for stuff, we are saying to God that we want what's in His hands, but not His heart. This is not a godly relationship; this is us attempting to barter with God. In this, we offer to serve Him in exchange for material things and worldly happiness. Therefore, what we are offering Him is servitude without the love, meaning, we are offering to serve Him without looking, thinking and behaving like Him. When we do this, we reject Him and by doing so, we cause Him to reject us. When God handed me a mirror, I cried and tossed it back at Him for many years, all the while complaining about never having experienced true love, always attracting the wrong folks and never having enough to get by. As my relationship with Him grew, I realized that I needed that mirror more than I needed my next breath. I took it and began to change what I saw. I didn't like what I saw, but knew I had to humble myself and make the changes that needed to be made if I wanted God's hand on every area of my life. This changed my life altogether and it changed my results BIG TIME. Let's not reject God's heart anymore. Embrace Him, get to know Him, and always be willing to pick up the mirror on your own and correct whatever it is that keeps you from looking like Him. Blessings are attracted to His likeness ... the more we look like Him, the more blessings will find and overtake us.

Sound of Fire 158

The soul (mind, will and emotions) are the belly of your life. They are centered around your thinking patterns, your choices and your perspective on life. A soul-tie is a linking of two or more souls, where each person influences the other's thinking patterns, choices and perspectives. That's why God told us not to be unequally yoked with unbelievers. An unbeliever is a person who has not allowed the Word to affect his or her mind, will or emotions. But because these arenas cannot go unoccupied, the devil influences those areas. When you link yourself up to an unbeliever, the devil, in a sense, places another "will" in your vehicle of life and he becomes an influence in your life.

Pay attention to how you think, feel and what you keep receiving in your life. They are indicative of what's behind the "will" of your soul.

Sound of Fire 159

Some doors have to be shut in order for others to open.

Sound of Fire 160
Jesus didn't make a way. He is the Way!

Sound of Fire 161
You can't love the hell out of somebody who loves their hell.

Sound of Fire 162
You cannot say that you're ready for marriage if you have conditions for divorce in your heart. If you say stuff like, "If he (or she) does _____, I will divorce him (or her)," you do not yet possess *Agape* love. A marriage built on *Eros* love cannot last because Eros is centered around romance. Without Agape (the greatest kind of love), Eros cannot stand the tests of time. That's why a lot of married women end up in "partnerships" with their husbands where romance is absent and everything is centered around control and manipulation.
Remove the conditions. You won't need them if God gives you away.

Sound of Fire 163
Repenting is not the same as apologizing.
Anyone can apologize.
A liar can apologize and still be a liar, meaning he or she will do it again, but a repentant soul cannot repent unless they are simultaneously agreeing to turn away from the sin AND turn back to God. Therefore, repenting involves a process. Apologizing is saying that you're sorry. Repenting is showing it.

Sound of Fire 164

We know what happens when sex is finished, right? There's a grand finale and the man loses his strength (which is why the Bible warns men to not give their "strength" to [immoral] women). The woman, on the other hand, receives an impartation which will result in a pregnancy and a birthing.
This is what happens when you sin.
Sin is death's womb.
In sin, you make an impartation.
When the time comes, sin gives birth to death, and it's your baby.
When you TRULY repent of sinning, you are terminating death's pregnancy.
If you do not repent, death will give birth once your grace period is up (God gives you a time to repent).
Don't play with sin. Sin is cute (sometimes) and it's fun (sometimes), but once it gives birth, you will not like what comes out of it.

Sound of Fire 165

We can become skilled at any and everything we do if we do it long enough. We can become skilled cooks, skilled drivers, skilled carpenters, etc. We can also become skilled manipulators, liars and sinners. That's why we have to repeatedly and intentionally serve God until it becomes our nature. That way, we change our default back to righteousness and we won't default to sin.

Sound of Fire 166

If you're asking God for a husband, you are asking God for a covering. The husband, according to the Word, is the head of the home. This means you are asking to be a responsibility as well as a help-meet. This also means that you must be responsible so that you can actually help your husband. Additionally, it means that the husband you end up with must know what he needs help with (purpose). One of the worst things we can do, as women, is desire to be something that we are not yet prepared for or desire to be with someone who is not yet prepared for us.

Sound of Fire 167

The entire purpose of holiness is so that you can look and sound so much like God that the enemy flees at the sight of your face or the sound of your voice.

Sound of Fire 168

Messed up mentality: Being excited about how loud you can make a man scream in the bedroom, but unable to get him to take you to the altar and whisper "I do."

Sound of Fire 169

Holiness is still right. If a man doesn't give you his last name, don't give him husband privileges.

Sound of Fire 170

Happy people attract happiness. People who love to be a blessing to others attract blessings. Loving people attract love. If you're asking God to send you something that you are not, you are asking Him to change the nature of His Word. It's the same as telling Him to cause darkness to give birth to light, or to cause an apple tree to bear watermelons. Be whatever it is that you want to attract.

Sound of Fire 171
Having sex with a man in exchange for his love is prostitution.

Sound of Fire 172
When someone judges you because of what you've gone through, they are only saying that they couldn't handle the weight of who God has ordained you to be!
Judgment from people is not offensive. It's actually a compliment.

Sound of Fire 173
Ungodly prayers aren't sent up; they are sent out.

Sound of Fire 174
You are a before and after snapshot. The question is ... can people see a remarkable difference or do they have to squint their eyes?

Sound of Fire 175
Sometimes, the one thing that's keeping you from tapping into God's yes is the fact that you won't give Him your yes. Relationships cannot be one-sided.

Sound of Fire 176

Have you ever seen a parent hand a newborn to a young child? If you have, did you notice how the parent made the child sit down first to keep him or her from dropping the infant? Even though the child may be asking to hold the infant, he or she is not strong enough or mature enough to hold the child. They would likely end up dropping the baby if they are not placed in a position where they can safely hold the baby.

God works the same way! When we ask Him for things, we have to be humble enough to receive them. That's why God tells us to humble ourselves; He wants to get us in a position where we can receive AND maintain whatever it is that we have been asking for. We cannot stand on the legs of pride and expect to be able to hold a God-sized blessing, even in its infancy. The reason is, we would drop it if we are not seated in humility. Whatever it is that you want, you need to humble yourself so God can trust you enough to hold it.

Sound of Fire 177

Proud people puff themselves up to appear bigger than what they are. Humble people shrink so that the greatness of God can be seen in them.

Sound of Fire 178

You can never justify sin to God; therefore, justifications are the manifestation of a people- pleasing spirit or a stiff neck.

Sound of Fire 179
You are what you notice the most. Ouch.

Sound of Fire 180
Your heart is always having a conversation with God outside of your intellect and religious reasoning. The question is—what is it saying?

Sound of Fire 181
Love will always lead you away from sin because God is love. Check the direction your relationship is leading you in. That way, you can tell if God is in it or not.

Sound of Fire 182
You can't bind the devil and serve him at the same time.

Sound of Fire 183
Ladies, the greatest love you can give your husband is by first learning to love God with all your heart, and then learning to wholly love yourself—flaws and all. You cannot ask a man to love you when you don't love yourself.

Sound of Fire 184
Man's "no" is just a stepping stool designed to help you get to God's "yes." When God gives it to you, no man can take it from you.

Sound of Fire 185
Religiousness is counterfeit holiness. It produces similar

sounds, but not the same results.

Sound of Fire 186
You don't have to defend yourself. Any weapon formed against you (when you're in right-standing with God) is a weapon formed against the call on your life. Because of this, it is a weapon formed against the One who called you and that's why it cannot and will not prosper.

Sound of Fire 187
It is possible for God-fearing people to talk you out of receiving a blessing if they don't understand the direction that God takes to get that blessing to you. After all, it's not for them to understand.

Sound of Fire 188
Be zealous in well doing, not jealous of those who do well.

Sound of Fire 189
You can be abstinent and still impure. Your heart determines your condition.

Sound of Fire 190
Ladies. You can pressure him to come to church, but you can't pressure him to come to Christ.

Sound of Fire 191
Your life is a testament to whatsoever god you serve.

Sound of Fire 192

Use your key! Anyone who enters in through the window is a thief!

Sound of Fire 193

The biggest problem with the average person is that he or she is average.

Sound of Fire 194

A boxer never lives in the same house as his or her opponent. Why? Because they don't want their opponents to know their strategies or have access to harm them before the big fight. They train in separate places and then they meet up in a mutually agreed upon arena to duke it out. Question is ... why would you want to live with the devil who opposes you? He is your opponent (even when you are on his side). If you allow him to dwell in your heart, he will fix the fight and you will lose ... every time.

In other words, you can't give place to the devil and expect to defeat him. You have to meet him wherever God sends you to confront him, and then you can easily overcome him.

Sound of Fire 195

Because I am the church, service (servitude) never ends.

Sound of Fire 196

If you open your ears and eyes to hear and see EVERYTHING relating to getting a husband, but are blind and deaf to the messages of holiness, you have made marriage an IDOL!

Sound of Fire 197

God holds us accountable for the whole truth, not just the truth we've accepted. We can't pick and choose which scriptures to follow and which ones to omit from our lives.

Sound of Fire 198

Culture =cult =occult. Be careful.

Sound of Fire 199

Understand this: when you say, "I do" to the wrong person, you may be saying, "I do" to the weapon that Satan has formed against you. That's like trying to cuddle with a rattlesnake.

Sound of Fire 200

When unholy people enter holy matrimony, they are always confronted by their own personal demons in an event that we call a storm. Guess how they handle the storm? They beat against each other with their words in an attempt to outperform the storm. When the storm leaves, it has done is far less damage to that marriage than the couple has done.

Chapter 3

Sound of Fire 201

If you desire to love a spouse, you must first love God more than you love yourself. If you don't, your reasoning for marriage will be centered around self and you will tear down your marriage with your own hands.

Sound of Fire 202

The solutions to many of this world's problems are in your womb. The people you have surrounding you are all midwives. The reason you haven't given birth to many of those solutions is because the people you have around you were sent by Pharaoh to kill whatsoever came out of your womb. So to protect you, God has to get you away from those folks before your baby can be born.

Sound of Fire 203

To pass some of God's greatest tests, you will have to fail many of the tests that people give you.

Sound of Fire 204

It's not about how many souls are coming to church. It's about how many souls are coming to Christ. Don't lose focus on the big picture.

Sound of Fire 205

Avoiding fornication isn't just planning to say "no." It's refusing to put yourself in a situation where your flesh can speak up on your behalf.

Sound of Fire 206

Sure, we tell and show God that we love Him, but we must also remember that He loves us.

Sound of Fire 207

Be who God designed you to be. Stop trying to redesign the masterpiece that you are!

Sound of Fire 208

God will have people interceding for you who you do not personally know! That's because they know you by the spirit!

Sound of Fire 209

Don't know what love is? Here's what the Bible says about love.

Love covers a multitude of sins.

Love is patient.

Love is kind.

Love does not envy.

Love does not boast.

Love is not proud.

Love does not dishonor others.

Love is not self-seeking.

Love is not easily angered.

Love keeps no record of wrongs.

Love does not delight in evil but rejoices with the truth.

Love always protects.

Love trusts.

Love always hopes.

Love always perseveres.
If one of these ingredients is missing, what you're witnessing is not love.

Sound of Fire 210

If someone comes to you and says, "Hey, we're going to be fasting for_____" and they ask you to join that fast, make sure you know the spirit of the person who launched it AND how they feel about the person they claim to be fasting for. You do NOT want to join in on something when you are unsure of the spirit that's behind it. Witches fast too, but they don't fast to God; they fast to familiar spirits.

Sound of Fire 211

People will test the strength of your backbone by trying to get you to make their enemies your enemies. This is manipulation and control; it is the very nature of the Jezebel spirit.

Sound of Fire 212

Holiness is true beauty in God's eyes.

Sound of Fire 213

It is possible to be married and lonely at the same time, especially if the person you marry cannot relate to you or vice versa.

Sound of Fire 214

Woman of God, one of the hindrances that keeps you from

being found by your God ordained spouse is unforgiveness. Why are you still mad at the man who walked out of your life? Don't you understand that God rejected that man as your husband, and that's why that man rejected you? It doesn't matter how bad he was to you; He is still a soul and God loves him. If you are in unforgiveness, you are still in a relationship with whomever you are have trouble forgiving, therefore, you are not free to be found. Let go and let what happened in that relationship serve as a lesson and a warning for you. Forgive.

Sound of Fire 215

It is possible for your favorite celebrities to die and end up in hell. Sure, we shouldn't want anyone to go to that place, but the truth is ... if Jesus Christ was not Lord OVER their lives or IN their lives, they won't make it through the pearly gates. After all, God is NOT a respecter of persons.

Sound of Fire 216

Woman of God,
You are not a toy-maker.
You are assigned as a help meet to your husband. You didn't have the tools to help the man (or men) you'd chosen for yourself; therefore, you used your tools to try to fix him (or them). There are Build-a-Bear workshops in just about every mall, but you tried to build a husband and then help him to be what you wanted and not who he really was. For this reason, you cannot complain about the men who walked away from you; after all, they were not assigned to your life.

Sure, you helped build them, but the truth is, before you started building, you had to tear them down. What you put in him was for you. It will work against his God-appointed marriage if he doesn't get delivered because the model of the man that you were building was not who he was designed to be. You are a daughter of the Most High God. As such, you should spend your time letting God build you up so that the man who was custom built by Him will find you. The only building you'll have to do in this man is to build him up when the enemy tries to tear him down. You will be his favor, his promotion and his motivation. When I was a child, I spoke and thought and reasoned as a child. But when I grew up, I put away childish things.

Sound of Fire 217
Sometimes, God won't let you connect with certain people simply because He knows you'll limit yourself to their potential.

Sound of Fire 218
The fear of God is like an electric fence. If you try to go outside of it, be prepared to get the shock of your life.

Sound of Fire 219
It is possible to never miss going to church and still miss God.

Sound of Fire 220
It is possible to memorize scripture and still end up in hell.

Sound of Fire 221

It is possible to delay meeting or courting your God-approved spouse simply because in your current state, God knows you won't approve of them.

Sound of Fire 222

On every level that we step onto and in every season that we step into, there will be a big box (limitations). On that box, are the words "NORMAL" and "TRADITIONS". In that box, you will find people who made it to that level and got tired of standing outside the box being talked about, yelled at and demonized from the people in the box. So, they boxed themselves into people's ideas of what they should do, what they should say, where they should go and how long they should be gone. In each box, there are a lot of smaller boxes, each representing a category. One box reads "Life in General", another box reads "Relationships", another one reads, "Ministry", and the list goes on. Each person, depending on where they were, has gone into his or her perspective box. From there, they were accepted and became a part of the norm. Eventually, they were given authority over every new person who entered the box. Their assignments were to ensure that nobody ever left the box. When a new person enters that level, the people who have authority over the folks in the box, went out to greet the ones who were outside of it. They were friendly, welcoming and generous, however, their jobs were to convince the folks to get in the box. Those who followed them into the box were given their uniformed thinking patterns, a name badge (the title their new leaders assigned to them) and an assignment (their purpose, according to the people who were leading them). They were to monitor other new converts and do whatsoever they had been assigned to do. Needless to say, there were some people who would not enter the box and this was offensive to the ones who were in it. This wasn't because the folks outside the box were bad; the problem was that those folks thought outside the box, and what happens outside the box will eventually affect what happens in the box. So, those nice, friendly and welcoming hosts suddenly began to snarl. This was because the folks outside the box were not subject to them or their rules. Because of this, those who ruled the box began to plot against the ones who stood outside the box. Nevertheless, they had only been given authority over the people in the box, so they could not do anything to the folks who lived outside of it! The point is ... in every new season, you will find a box with the words "NORMAL" and "TRADITIONS" on it. If you enter that box, you will get stuck in those seasons and you will have to follow the chain of command that has been assigned to the folks in the boxes. You will follow man's ranking system and your movement will be controlled by the folks who outrank you in the box. However, if you're willing to offend the norm, forsake tradition and stand outside the box, God will repeatedly promote you from one level to the next and nothing shall by any means harm you or stop you! You will not be subject to the man-made laws of the folks who live in the box! But if you can't stand to be talked about and you hate to stand out, you will find yourself in the box, waiting to be promoted by folks who you (not God) have given authority over yourself. They will rule over you and promote you from one wall to the next, but they will NEVER let you leave that box!

Sound of Fire 223
Most of the time when people tell lies on you, they do it to hide the truth about themselves.

Sound of Fire 224
The way up (promotion) is down (humility).

Sound of Fire 225
Love will take you further in life than money, fame and power.

Sound of Fire 226
People who aren't led astray by idle thoughts and selfish ambition forsake what is natural to embrace what is supernatural. This doesn't mean that they don't like nice things, but it does mean that they won't sell out to get or keep them!

Sound of Fire 227
Sometimes, the problem is—you're not desperate enough. When you get desperate for the enemy to leave you alone, you won't just pray him away; you will bind that serpent, chop off its head and send that spirit away defeated, overcome and regretting the day it came your way.

Sound of Fire 228

Sometimes, the issue isn't that God isn't hearing your prayers. The issue is you're praying with the wrong motives. Check your heart and your motives before lifting your voice to God, and if you find anything that shouldn't be there (offense, hurt, selfish ambition, pride, etc.), try giving that to God first and asking Him to deliver you from it. Once He does, you will find that your prayers will change because your heart has changed.

Sound of Fire 229

During the night, we have to turn the lights on in our houses so that we can see our way around the darkness. If we don't do this, we would stumble. Understand this: The storms will come. It is then that darkness is upon you and YOU MUST LET YOUR LIGHT SHINE IF YOU WANT TO AVOID STUMBLING. Complaining never lit up the night and crying about a storm never made it lift. Darkness is overcome by light and the temptation to complain is overcome by praise and worship.

Sound of Fire 230

Love conquered sin. Your victory is in love, but sin will defeat you if you love it.

Sound of Fire 231

Why do you keep chasing Eros (romantic love) when Agape (unconditional, Godly love) is chasing you?

Sound of Fire 232

Understanding is Heaven's translation of a revelation that's been interpreted so that you can chew it.

Sound of Fire 233

Everything that enters your heart has a root. To get rid of it, you need to pull it out by the root.

Sound of Fire 234

Love is a true story.

Sound of Fire 235

Your God-appointed wife will intercede for you instead of tearing you down.

Sound of Fire 236

Your God-appointed husband will cover you before uncovering you.

Sound of Fire 237

You are a sign and a wonder!

Sound of Fire 238

God sees and ministers to the best in you.

Sound of Fire 239

What worked yesterday should not work today. Move on.

Sound of Fire 240
Fear is faith in the devil.

Sound of Fire 241
When you throw a dart into the enemy's camp, you'd be amazed at who says "ouch."

Sound of Fire 242
The most potent and effective leader is one who'll forsake a platform to tell the truth.

Sound of Fire 243
Every season has a fragrance and a sound! Tune into your spiritual senses.

Sound of Fire 244
Life is more than experience. It's a series of revelations!

Sound of Fire 245
Stop allowing folks to tell you who to like, be friends with or love. That, in itself, is witchcraft in its baby stages.

Sound of Fire 246
New day, new mercies. Yesterday's mindset is now expired. Advance into today.

Sound of Fire 247
It is possible to have a house full of people and no one to talk to.

Sound of Fire 248
When we die to self, we take away Satan's most effective weapon against us: ourselves.

Sound of Fire 249
When you die to self, you are, in a sense, choosing to be absent from the lusts and desires your body to be present with the Lord. This means that you choose to let the super invade your natural and you will become a supernaturally charged vessel who not only speaks of the power of God, but demonstrates it.

Sound of Fire 250
Credit cards are Satanic invitations to bondage. Don't accept the invite.

Sound of Fire 251
Serving God is more than dancing around and shouting at church. It's more about what you do when no one can see you but God.

Sound of Fire 252
The root word of discipline is disciple. Without discipline, you cannot be God's disciple.

Sound of Fire 253
A storm in life oftentimes serves as a lie detector test. For example, people can give you what they think is love, but when the storms of life hit, their love does not withstand the

tests, meaning it was not love. It was flattery, tolerance, obsession, lust and the like. Understand this: Love never fails; that's biblical. This means that if someone fails to love you, they didn't love you in the first place. Understand what love is. Study the biblical definition of love so you can identify true love from the emotions and spirits that often masquerade themselves as love.

Sound of Fire 254
A man or a woman's capacity to love is subject to and measured by his or her understanding of what love is.

Sound of Fire 255
It is possible to walk out of a church building not knowing any more than what you knew when you walked into it.

Sound of Fire 256
A good tree cannot bear evil fruit!
Ladies, one of the fruits of a husband is that he is a protector. If a man comes along and tries to sleep with you outside the covenant of marriage, he is attempting to uncover without covering you, meaning he is not protecting you; he is exposing you to the enemy. This is NOT the fruit of a God-sent man! A husband is supposed to lead you in Christ Jesus and not away from Him. In other words, any man who tries to lead you into the bedroom before covering you as a husband is a man who is leading you AWAY from God. This is NOT the fruit of a good tree! Know this: A man will ALWAYS lead you to his father! The question is: Who's his daddy?

Sound of Fire 257
A wife is a help meet. A woman cannot be found by her husband until she is ready to help him. This means that a wife is NOT a woman sitting around waiting on some man to come and rescue her; after all, she needs help and therefore, could not be a help meet.

Sound of Fire 258
When God becomes number one in your life, everything else has no choice but to fall into order!

Sound of Fire 259
It is possible for a man to marry a woman he does not love simply because she lets him have his way. It's called an arrangement.

Sound of Fire 260
Any man can find a woman, but it takes a skilled godly warrior to find his own wife.

Sound of Fire 261
When God looks at your heart, He sees your real face. The question is ... how do you look to Him?

Sound of Fire 262
If there were two of you, would you want to be your friend?

Sound of Fire 263
Your finances have to go through deliverance too! Cast the

devil out of your finances and refuse to open anymore demonic access doors into your finances (example: credit cards, car notes, reckless spending).

Sound of Fire 264
Credit cards are nothing but demonic debit cards for the impatient.

Sound of Fire 265
If you're asking God to send you the God-appointed spouse, but you keep putting yourself in debt or putting yourself further in debt, you are working against what you've been praying for.

Sound of Fire 266
Love never fails. People just fail to love.

Sound of Fire 267
Dear Overcomers,
We are the Harriet Tubmans of spirituality. We don't just get saved for ourselves. We go back and rescue our brothers and sisters in the Lord!

Sound of Fire 268
Progress overcomes procrastination. If you keep planning to stop procrastinating, you're procrastinating to plan.

Sound of Fire 269
I am favor manifested.

Sound of Fire 270
Sometimes, being in the will of God means stepping outside the understanding of man.

Sound of Fire 271
If you don't tell the devil to "get thee behind me Satan" when he tempts you, the deliverance minister is going to have to tell him to come out of you! It is better to have the devil cast out of your presence than it is to have him cast out of you.

Sound of Fire 272
There's a difference between someone who calls you because they want to talk with you versus someone who calls you because they want someone to talk to.

Sound of Fire 273
God favors favor with favor.

Sound of Fire 274
You don't need anyone's permission to be as anointed as you are! God is not governed by board members; He does not need permission to bless you! Know this: Every religious poll designed to question your anointing is governed by hell itself!

Sound of Fire 275
God did not send out passive-aggressive prophets! True prophets are bold as a lion because they were sent to

confront, uproot and dismantle anything that is unlike God!

Sound of Fire 276
Woman of God ... You are a rose to the man who was sent by God to hold you, but you will be thorns to any other man who God has not given permission to touch you!

Sound of Fire 277
You will NEVER draw NEGATIVE attention from someone who's gone past you! When you awaken the critic, it's because you stepped on his toes when you went past him or her!

Sound of Fire 278
You're writing your life's story right now! Quick question: Will God want to put your life's book in His library or will it be a profane, blasphemous, pornographic story only fit for the flames? In this hour, we have to dig for the truth in order to uproot the lies ... We have to be honest with ourselves!

Sound of Fire 279
Worry is nothing but faith in the devil's abilities.

Sound of Fire 280
As we go through the seasons of life, we are introduced to new realities, new mindsets and new changes. Every season in your life preaches a sermon to you, but it's what you take from that sermon that will determine whether you are held back or promoted! Sudden changes in the seasons are not

always fun, especially when the new information conflicts with the old information. Nevertheless, the seasons of change are necessary for growth. Now, here's the issue. We have to have the Word deeply in us so that we can take from each season what we need to take from it, otherwise, we'll try to let new information run through old filters (thinking patterns). That's when we end up missing the potency of each season's sermon and we'll end up delayed, held back and bound! People who miss their season's sermon become "seasoned" in bondage.

Sound of Fire 281
Whatever you worry about, you empower.

Sound of Fire 282
Deliverance doesn't make people act better. It just takes away their excuses.

Sound of Fire 283
You can't sin your way into a storm and then praise your way out of it. Storms chase the rebellious, but the righteous have the right to silence them.

Sound of Fire 284
Don't get so caught up missing what you had that you end up missing what you have.

Sound of Fire 285
Any prayer sent out against God's will is called a witchcraft

prayer, even if you attempt to mask the prayer as a godly one. It doesn't matter what your intentions are; God looks at your motives! He looks at the intent and content of your heart! So, for example, if you pray that God takes away someone's wealth, car, health or happiness because you think they need to be humbled, you are operating as a witch, and as such, your prayers will fall upon yourself. You will watch from afar as God elevates, protects and enlarges the territory of the person you tried to pray against. You will watch your life fall apart, and your prayers will rise up just to fall back down until you repent of your ungodly ways! Stop praying from your angry place, your jealous place, your place of envy or your lack of understanding, and start asking the lord to set you free from all ungodly mindsets. If you don't, you'll end up praying the wrong prayers and they won't rise up to God, but they will land on the devil's desk. If the person you are attempting to pray against is covered by the blood, the wrath of God will fall upon your home because when you rise up against one His own, you rise up against him. And that's a war you cannot win!

Sound of Fire 286

Your love for YAHWEH will always be tested, not by God, but by the enemy. He will place people and things in front of you and try to get you to have an ungodly, idolatrous relationship with those things or people. He will then try to convince you that as long as you go to church, pray to the Lord and claim Him as your God that He will overlook your idolatry. Satan is a liar and the truth is not in him! Any person and anything you put before God is an idol and it is a manifestation of your ungodly relationship with your own reflection! Humble yourself and put God first, not just on Sundays and during prayer time—God has to be first all the time! When you exalt people and/or things over the Almighty God, you are, in the same, submitted to Satan because idolatry falls under his kingdom.

Sound of Fire 287
I will NEVER get to a place where I won't need God. I will always need Him, and more than that, I will always want Him. Relationships built on need are one-sided and unfair.

Sound of Fire 288
Love sees you for who you are, not what you were.

Sound of Fire 289
God's love for you is perfect; there are no flaws in it.

Sound of Fire 290
Give God the praises He's due and He will give you more reasons to praise Him.

Sound of Fire 291
The question isn't "Will God heal you?" He already did that—the question you should be asking is how to tap into to healing that He has set aside for you.

Sound of Fire 292
One of the worst positions to find yourself in is to be somewhere trying to disprove the Word of God by using the Word of God.

Sound of Fire 293
You cannot fortify what you have compromised.

Sound of Fire 294
Invention ideas, the cures to every disease and new advancements in technology ... they are all within our bellies, but it takes reaching for them to pull them out. The world, with its perverted heart, reaches within themselves and pulls out what God has stored in them, and then, they pervert it because they are perverted. As the church, we must pursue the intimate knowledge of God, and then reach within ourselves to pull out every idea and treasure that God has stored within us. That way, we can glorify God, distribute the wealth the way God wants us to and we can live the lives that God wants us to have.

Sound of Fire 295
When on a plane, the flight attendant normally says something that I find interesting. He or she says that should there be an emergency on the plane that requires a parent or parents to put on their oxygen masks or life vests, those parents should first put on and secure their own masks and vests before they attempt to put their children's masks and vests on them. The first time I heard this, I thought to myself

that no mother in her right mind would put her own safety before the safety of her children. It didn't take me long to realize the reason the airlines suggests this. If a parent attempts to secure his or her children's life vests and masks before securing his or her own, that parent may lose consciousness before he or she can save the life of his or her child or children. Children depend on their parents for survival; without the parent or parents, the likelihood of the child or children surviving is drastically decreased, especially if the kid is an infant or toddler. By saving his or her own life and securing himself or herself, the parent ensures that he or she is alive to save the life of his or her child or children. This is the same principle that we must apply in our journeys to salvation and then to holiness. We must get saved and secured in our own walks before we can effectively save others. If we don't, we may fall away (backslide) and cause many of the people who've come to the knowledge of God because of us, to perish with us. Some of these people would never have come to Christ because they didn't witness someone they thought was secure, pass away. They saw that person return to the very state that they were trying to get them to turn away from. We don't just get saved and start ministering to folks; we need renewed minds! We need to put on the mind of Christ so that when we try to secure others, we don't fall into temptation! Warfare comes when you first reach for salvation, but you will deal with a whole new level of warfare when you reach back in and try to save others! That's why you need to be rooted in the Word of God so that when the storms hit, you don't lose ground!

Sound of Fire 296

The objective is to learn the lesson, not become the lesson.

Sound of Fire 297

The person you are today should be wiser than the person you were yesterday. The days of the week change and so does the weather. If you're not doing the same, you have a lot of catching up to do.

Sound of Fire 298

Loving God is a whole new level of love because it requires that we love a God we've never seen. This is a fate that a standard believer cannot accomplish because loving God requires that we first believe that He exists. Then we must know Him personally and intimately. In other words, we have to step outside the norm. This means that we have to read His Word, spend time in prayer, and we must acknowledge His breath on every good thing. If we don't do this, we will speak of loving Him with our mouths, but our hearts won't bear witness with our words. God said that many will come before Him boasting of works (prophesying and casting out devils), but He will say, "Get away from Me for I never knew you." What does this mean? The people in question knew scriptures and they were aware of the existence of God, and yet they did not have an intimate relationship with Him. There was no alone time with Him; there was just a bunch of religiousness and performances but no true submission; after all, you cannot submit to a God whom you are not personally acquainted with. Submission requires intimacy. In other words, to spend eternity with God, we absolutely HAVE to know Him and love Him. This isn't accomplished by going to church, memorizing scriptures and speaking in tongues; these are all fruits of the Spirit, our love for Him or what we've come to believe. This is accomplished by coming outside of standard church practices and spending one on one time with God ... consistently. It is accomplished by involving God in your day-to-day life and being careful that you don't allow yourself to see Him as a genie who's only good for giving you what you want. We have to press into God's presence so that we can access a whole new level of love (one that we do not understand)—and we've got to stay there! Relationships require quality time, understanding AND selflessness in order to work. Without these three key ingredients, love doesn't come forward, but expectation does, and there's nothing worse than being in a relationship with someone who has a lot of expectations of you but no love for you!

Sound of Fire 299
We are imperfection trying to get back to perfection, but in order to do this, we have to remove everything we've placed before the Great I AM.

Sound of Fire 300
Love never fails and lust never wins.

Chapter 4

Sound of Fire 301

God said that He would give us the desires of our hearts; we understand this, but there is another layer to this. God will grant you the desires of your heart after He has changed it! You see, in our states of brokenness, we ask for void-fillers in the areas where we need wisdom, knowledge, understanding and deliverance! Had God sent us our supplies and desires in those states, we would not have had any incentives to come out of them! He knows what it takes to drive us out of old mindsets and into our destinies, so instead of complaining about what He has not done, how about you thank Him for what He has AND has not done?

Sound of Fire 302

When I was living in Florida, it was not uncommon for me to see black vultures. Anytime a black vulture saw a dead animal, it would sound the alarm and the other vultures would all gather around to consume the dead animal's carcass. When they saw a dying animal, they would hoover up in the sky near the area where the dying animal was. They would wait for the animal to expire and if the animal was still walking, they'd follow it patiently until it was too weak to go any further. In many cases, they'd start devouring the animal while it was still alive!

Do you realize that there are some people who, spiritually speaking, are nothing but dark vultures? They'll follow you around and even follow your ministry, but they are not doing this to show their support! They are waiting for the right opportunity to swarm in and accuse you, attack you, or, if they see you down—finish you off! It's sad, but this is the truth. Not everyone who says "I love you" loves you, just like not everyone who cries "Lord, Lord" will enter Heaven. Be prayerful because if you slip, the birds of prey will swoop in!

Sound of Fire 303

It is possible for someone to be popular and wrong at the same time. (example: Islamic leaders, Popes, etc.)

Sound of Fire 304

It is possible to correct someone and still not be assigned as that person's leader or covering. Brothers and sisters in the Lord are supposed to correct one another, but that does not mean that the person you corrected is your spiritual son or daughter.

Sound of Fire 305

It is possible to be single and happy—in the Lord.

Sound of Fire 306

You may love the sin, but it does NOT love you back! The wages of sin is death. In other words, sin is an employer that is constantly trying to hand you your last paycheck ... literally.

Sound of Fire 307

The worst thing you can do to the wrong man is make him pay for something he does not value. He won't buy it.

Sound of Fire 308
We have to be faith-filled before we can be faithful.

Sound of Fire 309
Prophets of God,
Be careful that you don't enter "people bondage" whereas you feel compelled to release a word regarding major events such as sports, elections, Powerball lotteries and so on. This happens when you receive the praise of man and forget to release that praise to God. From there, you become the people's prophet and you feel like you "owe" them a word anytime something major is coming up. If you miss the mark, you will then feel like you "owe" them an apology. This is people bondage. Your assignment is to watch, pray and release a Word that edifies the people of God in their relationships with God. Yes, sometimes, people will pull on you for a Word, but that doesn't mean you have to release one. Sometimes, all God wants you to do is rebuke the spirits in the person or people who are pulling on you for a Word because they are "tempting" you to speak when God has not spoken! That's because what's in them is trying to attack your name! Remember, "owe" no man nothing but to love him!

Sound of Fire 310
Rebellion is witchcraft disguised by religion.

Sound of Fire 311
It is possible for a man to love you and want to spend his life

with you, even though he's never had sex with you.

Sound of Fire 312
Credit cards sell bondage to impatient people.

Sound of Fire 313
Every time you place yourself in debt, you become a slave of the people you owe!

Sound of Fire 314
You can't make a real difference until you have been changed!

Sound of Fire 315
Life is like a chess game. Your next move is based on where you are now, what you're currently facing and where you're trying to go. If you spend your life worrying about the movements of other people, your perspective will never grow up (perspectives are like children; as we age, endure and overcome, our perspectives shift and mature because our positions change). This helps us to be more loving and understanding to others regardless of their perspective because we come to understand that they are simply at a different place in their lives and walks; that's it and that's all. When you can't respect another person's perspective, it's likely because you cannot relate to their positioning. If you accept (or have accepted) the call to ministry, God will shift your thinking by changing your positioning CONSTANTLY—especially if He wants to use you in a major

way. This is because He understands that you won't be sensitive to hearing from folks who don't look like you, serve like you or preach like you. Oftentimes, when this happens, we say that we're being attacked when, in truth, we are being re-positioned so that we can change our perspective!

Sound of Fire 316
There are some saints who say, "It don't take all that" and then there are some saints who will do all that it takes to please God.

Sound of Fire 317
You can't hate wisdom and expect promotion!

Sound of Fire 318
Your life is a story that will someday be read back to you.

Sound of Fire 319
Sexual perversion is the lust of the heart manifested in the flesh! It is when sin rules a person's mind and limbs.

Sound of Fire 320
There is a wisdom available for us that most people won't tap into because they are afraid of it! Press your way on in!

Sound of Fire 321
Respect the seasons and you will learn from them.

Sound of Fire 322
There is a season for everything underneath the sun. Make peace with that truth and your life will be much easier.

Sound of Fire 323
Where is the will of God in your storm? It's wherever peace is.

Sound of Fire 324
Tomorrow is a continuation of today so make sure that what you want to follow you into tomorrow is not killed by whatsoever followed you into today.

Sound of Fire 325
When the wrong person rejects you, that person has just complimented you. Think about it.

Sound of Fire 326
Stop questioning God's will and just get in it.

Sound of Fire 327
We all have a LOT to be thankful for, but many of us forget to give thanks.

Sound of Fire 328
Keep your love, saints. It's the most powerful weapon you have besides, of course, the Word of God. If the enemy can take your love, he can take your power.

Sound of Fire 329

The truth is ... hell is full of good people who did almost everything right, but refused to forgive someone. Unforgiveness is nothing but an umbrella—whoever you're mad at, you are covering! You are volunteering to take whatever is thrown their way because you want to deliver what you feel is their just reward. Stop it! Release people as soon as they offend you. Love won and anytime you step out of love, you sit in the loser's seat! Check your heart and if there is someone you're angry with, forgive them and release yourself!

Sound of Fire 330

Regardless of who you are, where you've been and where you're heading, God still loves you. Build on that.

Sound of Fire 331

Just trust God. He hasn't failed you yet and He's not about to fail you now. He is faithful. I'm a living witness.

Sound of Fire 332

When a man finds a wife, he finds a good thing and obtains favor from the Lord. The problem these days is too many (unchanged) men are finding women; when the two get married, one becomes a married man and the other a married woman. There's a difference between a married man and a husband just as there is a difference between a married woman and a wife.

Sound of Fire 333

A help meet who doesn't know how to help is almost as bad as a help meet who doesn't know who to help.

Sound of Fire 334

Some people get so caught up in other people's opinions that they fail to develop their own.

Sound of Fire 335

You need faith for EVERYTHING ... even to doubt God! To doubt God means that you believe or have faith in something or someone else! Even atheists have faith, but their faith is perverted and misplaced; they have faith in science and men, both of which have proven to be faulty.

Sound of Fire 336

Some people make good spouses because they've witnessed loving, strong marriages between their parents. Then again, there's the other 50% who want loving, God-filled relationships, but don't know how to have them. Truthfully, in this bunch, (I believe) there has to be a humbling, otherwise, people go into marital unions with unrealistic expectations and no longsuffering. In other words, (I believe) people who've never seen love demonstrated, oftentimes have to be humbled by bad relationships before they can appreciate good ones.

Sound of Fire 337

You haven't been tested until you were at a point when it

was easier for you to fail than it was for you to pass.

Sound of Fire 338

Your lowest point in life should be when you offer God the highest level of praise. It's what you do when you're down that will determine the level of promotion God can entrust you with.

Sound of Fire 339

That deep, wretched feeling you get in your belly when you're about to do something wrong is your spiritual stop sign. If you run it, don't be surprised at what you run into or what (spiritually speaking) runs into you!

Sound of Fire 340

Your God-purposed spouse will complement you, but the wrong person will compliment you. What's the difference? Complement is a state of being; it is the very nature of a thing, but the word compliment represents mere words; things spoken, but not necessarily believed or meant.

Sound of Fire 341

A mature child of God who goes after an unsaved person or a babe in Christ is a spiritual pedophile.

Sound of Fire 342

Love is the dialect of God's people; it is the language of the Kingdom of God. We speak love fluently. Satan's children speak a few words of love, but their forked tongues won't allow them to speak the language of love. That's why their accents betray them when controversy hits.

Sound of Fire 343

Never complain about a problem that you're not willing to do anything about.

Sound of Fire 344

A child's eyes are innocent. God's eyes are holy. Whatever you wouldn't subject a child to, you shouldn't subject God to.

Sound of Fire 345

Human beings are creatures of adaption who hate change, even though it is necessary for growth. What I'm saying here is ... people can spend their lives with individuals they do not love (or like, for that matter) simply because they do not want to disturb their comfort zones. Don't end up romantically tolerated by a glorified roommate just because you got tired of waiting on God. The worst spouse to have isn't a cheater (surprise, surprise); the worst spouse to have is someone who faithfully despises you, but plans to stick around because they don't think they can do any better.

Sound of Fire 346

Every choice you've made was once a seed that started as a thought, which then rooted itself in the heart and bloomed into an action. In other words, your life and everything in it is a manifestation of your heart's condition.

Sound of Fire 347

The spirit of rejection opens the door for the spirits of jealousy and envy. When you have a rejected soul in your camp, that person will try to keep you from any form of advancement because he or she will fear losing you as a friend should God call you forward without them. It's not that they are wicked souls plotting to take over your world. Oftentimes, the issue is you have become their world and this, in itself, is dangerous.

Sound of Fire 348

Stop trying to be a Mrs. to someone who should be calling you Ma'am.
Stop trying to be a husband to someone who should be calling you Sir.

Sound of Fire 349

Saints, let go of the world before you get what's coming to them.

Sound of Fire 350

It is possible for someone to do evil things to you, go out of their way to break you, repent and end up in heaven while you end up in hell because you refused to forgive them.

Sound of Fire 351

It is possible to have spent your whole life going from one relationship to another and never have experienced being truly loved by a person. People who do this oftentimes fear love and run at the first sight of it.

Sound of Fire 352
People of God, study the ways, nature and heart of love if you desire to be married. Too many people get married wanting to be loved, but not knowing how to sincerely love someone outside of the bedroom and the kitchen. Love stands up and takes out pride whenever it rises up, but if you don't have genuine, Agape love, your pride will swallow up the measure of love that you do have and your marriage will follow suit.

Sound of Fire 353
A seductress is nothing but a glamorous witch whose witchcraft is found in her words and in the powers of her body. Even though she's not chanting or speaking curses over people, she is still a witch.

Sound of Fire 354
For the married: it is possible for a marriage to survive adultery if the adulterer truly repents. Don't give up just because it's popular to do so.

Sound of Fire 355
It is possible to delay meeting your God-assigned spouse simply because you're ready for the better, but not the worse. You can spend your days talking about what you will not take off a man or woman and end up delayed simply because you're admitting to God and yourself that you do

not possess longsuffering.

Sound of Fire 356
It is possible to live in this world and not be a part of it.

Sound of Fire 357
When a man or woman of God attacks an idol, those who worship that idol will feel it.

Sound of Fire 358
It is possible to enter a soul-tie with a person whom you have never had sex with. There is such a thing as emotional soul-ties. Consider David and Jonathan.

Sound of Fire 359
When millionaires invest in something and does not receive a return on their investments, they don't stop investing simply because they have suffered a loss. Instead, they learn how and where to invest; in other words: they get smarter! Most millionaires and billionaires have invested much and lost much, but they did not give up! The message here is ... it is possible to keep loving the wrong people the right way and lose. This doesn't mean you should stop loving; instead, you need to invest more love in God and yourself; that way, when your God-approved spouse comes, you can go for broke and invest more love and more trust into that relationship than you did in the previous ones. It is that level of faith that separates the bitter from the better.

Sound of Fire 360

It is possible to be denied entry into your wealthy place simply because you keep coveting someone else's wealthy place.

Sound of Fire 361

It is possible to delay connecting with the right people simply because you refuse to fully disconnect from the wrong ones.

Sound of Fire 362

It is possible for a leader to be rich and still be in the will of God.

Sound of Fire 363

It is possible for a leader to take up a huge offering and still be in the will of God.

Sound of Fire 364

The greater the sacrifice, the greater the reward.

Sound of Fire 365

Saints, you ARE the church. You bring God into the building; the building does not put God in you! Understand this: not everyone who's in the building screaming and singing is praising YAHWEH! Some folks are praising religious imaginations of who they think God is! YAHWEH is our Creator, but some people have created their own versions of Him and they praise the creature (created thing) more than the Creator because they have created an idol, tagged it with

God's name and they come to the sanctuary to worship it! They stand beside you, lifting up their voices and weeping to their god and if you're not careful, they'll have you praising the mental images they've created. That's why it is imperative that you understand that you ARE the church. That way, you can bring EL SHADDAI with you, and when they stand next to you worshiping a false god, the Lord Mighty in battle can get their attention. You are the church! Now act like it!

Sound of Fire 366

One of the reasons so many people stay frustrated is because they keep trying to reason with demons. I tell you the truth when I say if you keep on living, you'll find out soon enough that demons are on their best behavior when they're bound!

Sound of Fire 367

There is a difference between an Ahab and a Eunuch. An Ahab is a person who had power from God, but relinquished that power to Jezebel, thus giving Jezebel legal authority over God's people. A Eunuch is a person who has been castrated (made a slave to Jezebel) since birth; a person who has no real power. Ahabs are oftentimes loyal followers of their Jezebels, but Eunuchs usually follow their Jezebels grudgingly because they are being forced (through fear, familiarity, coercion, etc.) to serve them. That's why Jezebel is always cast off the wall by her Eunuchs after she loses her Ahab in battle, thereby losing the authority that was once given to her by Ahab. Eunuchs are oftentimes loyal to Ahab, but once Ahab is gone, Jezebel is left powerless and surrounded by people who hate her.

Sound of Fire 368

Oftentimes, an Ahab'ed female is nothing but a Jezebel in training.

Sound of Fire 369

There are some mornings when the enemy will be waiting for you at your bedside. The way you shut that down is to praise God before you get out of bed.

Sound of Fire 370

If Satan has never tried to stop you, it's because you were already headed in the wrong direction. If Satan has never tried to tear you down, it's because you were already standing on the wrong foundation. If Satan has never tried to defame your character, it's because your character is already promoting his kingdom. Pay close attention to your challenges. They'll tell you whether you're a threat to the enemy or his ally.

Sound of Fire 371

The struggle is just what it is ... a struggle. It's when you stop struggling and learn to live with your strongmen that you ally yourself with the enemy. You're either fighting against Satan or fighting with him; there are no neutral places in this battle. When you stop struggling, you'll start saying things like, "God knows my heart," and "Nobody's perfect." That's because we will ALWAYS try to justify being wherever we've settled down mentally and spiritually! If you've learned to live with your strongmen, you will try to convince others and yourself that the place you're in is a good place, a God-approved place or a God-assigned wilderness. Stop it! You need to struggle with whatever's struggling with you until you learn how to tap in to your "more than a conqueror through Christ Jesus" status.

Sound of Fire 372
Love makes the difference and that's why people who choose love over hatred make a difference.

Sound of Fire 373
Create an atmosphere that attracts God.

Sound of Fire 374
Today, you can encourage somebody or tear someone down. Whatever words you choose, just remember, tomorrow you'll reap from them.

Sound of Fire 375
The heart of an intercessor is made evident in times of peril.

Sound of Fire 376
Your arms can only reach so far ahead of you, but your faith should reach the nations.

Sound of Fire 377
Love is an impenetrable covering. Stay in love.

Sound of Fire 378
Pray for those who are praying against you. Trust me, they will need it.

Sound of Fire 379
Let righteousness be your garment and praise be your fragrance. That's how you attract the favor of God.

Sound of Fire 380
Peace, be still! In other words, peace is found in your stillness! Let God be God, and your job is to simply to obey Him. Everything else is God's business!

Sound of Fire 381
When I was unpacking, I found an old set of keys. I couldn't remember what they had been used for, but what I did know was that it made no sense for me to hold on to them. They represented an old life I once lived. They once opened doors that I needed to enter; they once started vehicles that got me from one place to another, and they locked away the things that mattered to me the most. Now, they are nothing more than a useless bunch of metal pieces that hold no value to me.

The same goes in relationships. Here's the truth. The average person stays bound to people who represent who they once were and not who they are today. They hold on because of familiarity; they hold on because closing old doors represent coming out of their comfort zones (places they've mastered) and walking into the peculiar (places where they need guidance). It's hard for an old police officer who can perform his duties blindfolded to adjust to being an FBI agent because he can no longer use old knowledge. Now, he has to rely on others to teach him to perform in his new role. But that's just it! God WANTS us to lean on Him and that's why He takes us out of our comfort zones and into new places where we can no longer rely on our old knowledge.

As I was looking for a remote to one of my televisions, I came across those old keys again and I've decided to toss them away because I'M NOT GOING BACK TO WHERE I ONCE WAS ... EVER! You need to do the same with people, old relationships and situations. Let go! It's time for you to stop trying to unlock new doors with old keys!

Sound of Fire 382
I don't use the "God knows my heart" rebuttal. I ask God to change my heart daily.

Sound of Fire 383
It is possible to be soul-tied to a person while that person has no ties to you!

Sound of Fire 384
If you refuse to forgive a person who's hurt you, you are (in the same) refusing to end your relationship with that person. Why ask God to send you a spouse when you're still holding

on to someone else?

Sound of Fire 385

The relationship we have with sin is an abusive relationship. How is it that we can divorce our spouses for abusing us, but can't seem to separate ourselves from sin? The answer is simple: People love their sin, but tolerate everyone else, including God!

Sound of Fire 386

Stop trying to prove yourself to people who need you to prove yourself to them.

Sound of Fire 387

When a man decides to make you his wife, he has either given you the highest honor in his life or the lowest place in his life, depending on where he is spiritually. Let's be honest ... not all men (or women) respect the people who dare to love them. With some people, the lowest rank you can have in their lives is to be their lovers or their spouses. Some men won't marry a woman simply because they feel she's too good for them, but they will marry a woman who they feel can take everything they are going to dish out. Such men look for women who wear their pain well ... women who can bounce back after every blow because they know they're going to be a handful. When my ex and I started going through a divorce, he stopped by my house one day and said something to me that I will never forget. He said, "Honestly, you're too good of a woman for me." I can't say that I was surprised at his words because everyone he surrounded himself with used and misused him and I'd spent most of our marriage trying to help him see how valuable he was (and is) to God. You see, he understood what it would take to be his wife. He understood that he was going to take whatever woman he was with through a whole lot of storms and he needed a woman who could weather them with little to no resistance. I have even heard some of my male relatives speak of women, saying that they were "too good" for them. What they're saying is that the women in question do not deserve what they are going to put their soul-tied lovers through! Ladies, men do recognize if they are a piece of work and when they're not ready or willing to repent, they will look for women who can withstand the storms that they are! So, don't be flattered every time a man flirts with you. If he's a God-fearing man who understands the value of a wife, he has just complimented you with one of the highest regards a man can adorn a woman with. If he's an ungodly, two-timing soul, his flirtation is the equivalent of him cursing you out. He's basically saying that he thinks you can (and deserve to) handle the storm that he is. Don't be flattered; grab your umbrella and walk away.

Sound of Fire 388

When you become a part of an idle man's world, you become part of an idle man's business. Don't get mad because he's always minding you.

Sound of Fire 389

Truthfully, having an unforgiving heart is the same as having a God complex. When you think someone's offense against you is punishment-worthy or hell-worthy, you end up qualifying for the same pit you've allowed your heart to dig for that person.

Sound of Fire 390

If you haven't met too many people of different races, more than likely, every time you see people of a certain race, they will look alike to you. Without relationship, everyone looks the same. Ladies and gentlemen, you need to understand this: without a relationship with God, you will see everyone who reminds you of another person in the same way. As a matter of fact, you'll create mental labels and mislabel people based on your experiences and the limitations of your understanding. Because of this, you will likely turn away people who have a genuine heart towards you, simply because they remind you of someone whose heart towards you was everything but good. The same goes in relationships. If you end up with an unsaved character, you will be nothing more than just another man or woman to that character; only he or she will have direct access to you. This access will allow them to mislabel you up close and personal, simply because people who don't have relationships with God don't venture too far outside of the familiar. That's why they'll tag you with personalities that you don't have and accuse you of things that is not in your nature to do. A relationship with God is necessary, otherwise, you give blind folks the keys to drive you around, and the only thing they'll do is drive you crazy!

Sound of Fire 391
If you forgive the puppet, you can effectively fight the puppet's master.

Sound of Fire 392
Contrary to popular belief, unforgiveness isn't a war against a person; it's a war against the very nature of who God is: love. Ironically enough, you could allow someone else's offense to cause you to offend God, meaning the enemy can successfully recruit you to his side by showing you what he says are the benefits of unforgiveness. But if you look at the small print, you'll see that the only one losing in unforgiveness is you. Don't let your storms be the training grounds that the enemy uses to teach you how to war against God. Instead, take your eyes off the offense, look directly into the eye of the storm and demand that it release the wisdom within it. Storms are treasure chests full of wisdom and opportunities; you just have to find your peace in the midst thereof to see them.

Sound of Fire 393
Satan has his own match-making show, but all of the contestants are losers.

Sound of Fire 394
There is a love that's greater than the love you've

experienced and that's why you need to press in to the presence of God all the more. Don't end up settling for a distant relationship with God; go closer to Him so you can experience true intimacy with Him. It is then and only then that you'll know what it's like to be truly filled.

Sound of Fire 395
Though he be in pain, a boxer needs to recover quickly after he's been hit. He has two choices: he can focus on the fight or he can focus on the pain. If he focuses on the pain, he'll lose the fight, but if he focuses on the fight, he'll likely take home the win and he can deal with the pain later.
Here's a message for you. Even though the enemy attacked you and many of his darts hurt, don't focus on the pain or what you stand to lose; focus on what's on the other side of the win. You have plenty of time to consider what you lost, but once you take home the victory, you'll be more focused on what you've gained.

Sound of Fire 396
Stop trying to unlock new doors with old keys!

Sound of Fire 397
There are flowers that grow in extreme conditions. Of course, they survive storms and climates that other flowers would not survive. In other words, don't complain about the many storms you've endured. Just be thankful that you're built to withstand them.

Sound of Fire 398

Your trials will either make you bitter or they'll make you better.

Sound of Fire 399

I choose love, integrity, loyalty, forgiveness, understanding, patience and all the "gifts" that truly make me rich. I couldn't imagine being any other way.

Sound of Fire 400

There's a difference between a visitor, a guest and an intruder. A visitor is someone who visits you. Most visitors are welcomed by their hosts. A guest is someone who is temporarily lodging with you. Like visitors, most guests are invited; they are extended stay visitors. And then, there is the intruder. The intruder is not welcome, therefore, he or she is trespassing. This means that he or she has committed a crime. Understand this: demons are either visitors (you keep inviting the people bound by them over through media or associations), guests (they are attached to and lodging in or with you because of your rebellion) or intruders (they don't have the legal right to touch, attack, visit or confront you). If you're in rebellion, your demons can bind and stay with you because you invited them in as guests through your sin. If you're in submission to God, the enemy doesn't have the right to put his hands, powers or witchcraft on you, meaning you can easily bind (arrest) every demonic intruder who does. If you're watching devil-inspired shows, listening to sin-promoting music or associating with ungodly people in ungodly ways, you are allowing the enemy to visit you every time you open your heart and ears to him. It won't be long before he becomes an extended stay guest. Know where you are in the Lord so you can fight the powers of darkness effectively, and if you're in rebellion, repent and come from under the devil's authority. You can't bind the devil if you keep inviting him over!

Chapter 5

Sound of Fire 401

Be encouraged. Your story doesn't end with what people say about you; it starts with what God says about you.

Sound of Fire 402

Sometimes, we'll enter a place looking to get blessed, but instead, God will require us to make a sacrifice in that place. If your motives are impure, your heart won't pass the test and you won't be a blessing. Instead, you'll whimper, whine and complain, and from there, walk away empty handed, or worse, walk away with ONLY what you went in to get. In other words, verily you will have received your reward, and even though that may sound good, it's not; it's actually pretty scary. If your motives are pure, your sacrifice will become a seed designed to give you greater than what you were hoping and praying for. Don't approach God looking for earthly things; always approach Him with the right heart and mind or at least ask Him to give you a right heart and a right mind; that way, when you enter a place, you walk in looking to be a blessing. That's when you'll walk out of that placed blessed. Even when your hands are empty, your heart will be filled.

Sound of Fire 403

Forgiving others is the same as getting out of God's way so that when He deals with them, He won't have to deal with you to get to them.

Sound of Fire 404
Love is an effective weapon.

Sound of Fire 405
Stop waiting on people to encourage you and start encouraging yourself in the Lord! David did it!

Sound of Fire 406
We see and experience what we need to see and experience because one day, we'll be a part of someone else's experience and we need to be ready when that person comes.

Sound of Fire 407
Remember this: God has a plan, even when you don't know what it is.

Sound of Fire 408
You will always know where God is moving in your favor based on the amount of warfare you get in that area.

Sound of Fire 409
Daddy God adorns His babies with His love, protection, favor, grace and wisdom. These garments are expensive, but Jesus has already paid the price for them.

Sound of Fire 410
Dear Church,
You don't have to look or sound like the world to draw the

world. You need to look and sound like the Lord. If you draw them using familiarity, you are drawing them through the use of familiar spirits. We don't conform to the world; they have to be transformed by the renewing of their minds!

Sound of Fire 411

Because I understand what an enemy is, if you don't want yours ... I'll take him/her! Footstools represent elevation and the more footstools you have, the higher you're permitted to go! You don't have to build the Tower of Babel when you have footstools because God will permit you to be elevated by the hands of your enemies!

Sound of Fire 412

If David hadn't confronted Goliath, he wouldn't have been promoted. Confront your giants and stop running from them.

Sound of Fire 413

There are some gossiping, lying Jezebels in the church who spend their days contemplating whose name they are going to defame. That's because their own names are not known! They slither close to God's people and try to learn as much as they can about their intended prey. After God exposes them for who and what they are and the believer distances himself or herself from them, the Jezebel's new focus is to attack the name and character of the person he or she was assigned to assassinate. Nevertheless, this ploy NEVER works. Instead, the Jezebel goes from one leader to the next—exposing himself or herself for what he or she truly is. If a leader wrestles with jealousy, insecurity or is undelivered in any area of his/her flesh, the Jezebel will play into that leader's weakness and accuse his/ her escaped (and delivered) prey of being the very thing that the leader in question loathes or wrestles with. By doing this, the Jezebel isolates and divides the church because that demon cannot operate where there is unity! That's why you should never be a part of a church that is divided! If you see division in the church, please know that Jezebel is there! Those who have ears will HEAR WHAT THE LORD IS SAYING. Those who lean to their own understandings will hear what Jezebel is saying. Jezebel is on the prowl, but the only way to defeat that demon is to repent of your sins (thus taking away its legal authority), submit yourself to God, and then test the spirit!

Sound of Fire 414
Some of your greatest characteristics were born in the fire of a trial. Why again do you despise trials?

Sound of Fire 415
You should NEVER speak of someone whom you have never intimately spoken with or prayed for. One of the biggest issues I've seen in the body is a bunch of assuming Christians who label what they do not understand. Because of this, many end up missing the very opportunities that God has presented for them simply because they didn't like the packages that their blessings came wrapped in. Understand this about God ... He does not send blessings wrapped in familiarity; he is a peculiar God!

Sound of Fire 416

I'm an opportunist; I say this all the time. I see opportunities in every good thing and in every bad thing. I see lessons and wisdom in everything. Most of all, I see how to take those lessons and the wisdom and turn them into something that will help the body of Christ. I'm an opportunist and every weapon formed against me presents another opportunity for me.

Sound of Fire 417

One sure fire way to know if you are dealing with a Jezebel spirit is if the person you suspect has it has trouble repenting. Jezebels HATE true repentance! It is easier to spoon with an angry bobcat and not get killed than it is to get a Jezebel to repent. With Jezebel, you are ALWAYS at fault and any errors on their part is simply backlash or a response to something you've done. Sure, Jezebels will apologize, but it's false humility! That's because the Jezebel spirit is married to pride and the two are inseparable!

Sound of Fire 418

You can let evil people provoke you to do bad things or inspire you to do great things.

Sound of Fire 419

Never reopen doors that God has shut!

Sound of Fire 420

Dear Joseph,

Because of the call on your life, you can't have just anyone around you ... especially your siblings! Wait until you arrive at your predestined place and God will shut the mouths of the naysayers, expose all the liars and give you the very provision your enemies need! But because you have God's heart, you will recognize that even though they lied on you, persecuted you and tried to separate you from your Father, they are still your brethren. You will love without measure and you will help them in their hour of need.

Sound of Fire 421
What doesn't define you has no choice but to refine you.

Sound of Fire 422
What we take from life determines what we put back in it and what we ultimately get back out of it. Life can be a wonderful circle of blessings or a vicious cycle of hurt. You decide.

Sound of Fire 423
I can walk up to three women and say, "Do good and good will follow you," and every last one of those women will likely receive the message differently. One woman may hear me saying that if she does well, good things will follow her— and she is right! Another woman may hear me saying, "It's because you've been doing wrong that evil keeps following you!" The third woman may hear me saying, "You are exempt from the Word, but everyone else must do well to receive good tidings. Nevertheless, you, on the other hand,

are perfect!" What determines what each woman hears is the conditions of their hearts. The one who heard what I was truly saying is a positive soul who has not allowed life to harden her heart and darken her perceptions. The second woman is a negative soul who, because of the many hurts in her life, sees me as another threat and thus sees the need to defend herself against her perception of me. The last soul has created a religious force-field around herself, and somehow believes that because God knows her heart, she's exempt from the Word of God. In her eyes, there has to be some illegible small print in the Word that allows for people in her situation to never be negatively impacted by the Word.

Which soul are you?

Sound of Fire 424

Life is a series of lessons and opportunities. It's what you take from the lessons of life that determines which opportunities are presented to you and who (God or Satan) presents those opportunities to you.

Sound of Fire 425

In order to do great and marvelous things in this life, you have to be willing to be hated, persecuted, misunderstood, mishandled and ostracized. No worries, though. These things won't define, affect or move you unless you let them. Instead, if you open your eyes and see them for what they really are (steps on your footstools) you'd rejoice and keep climbing.

Sound of Fire 426
Desire becomes lust when it overrides your thoughts and influences your actions. In other words, any feelings that have the power to move you instead of being moved by you, is demonic!

Sound of Fire 427
A woman who knows her worth is FAR more confident than a woman who trusts in her feminine wiles. That's because her confidence is in the Lord and He has shown her what she is worth to Him. He has placed a price tag on her, and if she truly believes that she's worth the astronomical price that's on that tag, no devil in hell can move her! Believe God when He says YOU ARE PRICELESS!

Sound of Fire 428
The only blessings Satan has are the ones he's stolen from people. Don't let him take what belongs to you and then offer it back to you for a fee that you simply cannot afford (your life, soul, health, abundance, peace, etc.).

Sound of Fire 429
The lives we live are nothing but a manifestation of what we believe!

Sound of Fire 430
Love is most effective when it is undeserved. Love your enemies.

Sound of Fire 431
Misunderstandings are oftentimes missed opportunities.

Sound of Fire 432
When people can't disqualify you, they'll try to discredit you. Nevertheless, fret not. When you're in the will of God, any attempt to tarnish your name is an attempt to cancel out your assignment, which means that the attack is demonic. In other words, the attack is against God and therefore cannot prosper!

Sound of Fire 433
What would you call a prisoner who sat in his cell day after day with the keys to freedom in his hand? You'd call him blind! How many saints are sitting in bondage with the keys to freedom in their mouths? Open your mouth and free yourself!

Sound of Fire 434
There's a difference between lust and desire. Desire is a healthy sexual appetite that can easily be ignored or overcome, but lust is an ungodly appetite of the flesh (normally brought on by a demonic spirit) that will not be ignored. Lust roots itself deep in the heart and presents itself as "an issue of life." Because it roots itself in the heart, unlike desire, it cannot be cast down; that spirit has to be cast out! Lust overwhelms the person who is bound by it ... so much so that they oftentimes give in to it.

Sound of Fire 435

Freedom starts with a renewed mind and a determination to stay free, meaning if you're addicted to porn, you'll destroy your porn collection and be proactive about ensuring that you don't watch anymore porn. If you're addicted to masturbation, you'll be proactive. One good thing to do is put hot sauce on your hands before you go to bed; that is, until your mind changes and living a pure life becomes a habit! If you're addicted to sex, you'll stay away from fornicators. You'll end relationships that are valuable to you to build upon a more important relationship, and that is your relationship with Christ Jesus.

Sound of Fire 436

Error: The truth shall set you free.
Truth: The Truth (Jesus Christ) has ALREADY set you free!

Sound of Fire 437

God's mouthpieces don't just tell you the truth you want to hear; they tell you the truth you NEED to hear! With that being said, ask yourself this: Am I God's servant (standard Christian) or am I His faithful servant (supernatural manifestation wrapped in flesh, but not led by flesh)?

Sound of Fire 438

It is foolish to marry a man and then use his spiritual condition as justification for not submitting to him. That's a Jezebel move! If you marry him, you must submit to him. But wait! I already know that there are a few of you who are saying, "I ain't submitting to no unsaved man!" First off, the Bible told you not to marry him in the first place, but if you did it anyway, you CHOSE that man as your head—or better yet, your LEADER. If he is uncovered (without Christ), you CHOSE a godless man to be your covering ... period! Israel wanted a king and they got Saul. They couldn't use Saul's rebellious ways to justify not submitting to the authority that they relinquished to him! They wanted him, so they got him! Secondly, the Bible did not state that a wife must submit to her "saved" husband, but that she is free to be a Jezebel with her unsaved husband; it told believing wives to submit to their husbands (period). The man's spiritual condition isn't mentioned because God told us to not yoke ourselves with unbelievers. He didn't say, "Just in case you don't obey me and you marry an unbeliever anyway, here's plan B." No! God gives two commandments to individuals who are married to unbelievers and they are:

1. 1 Peter 3:1: "Wives, in the same way submit yourselves to your own husbands so that, if any of them do not believe the word, they may be won over without words by the behavior of their wives"... and

2. 1 Corinthians 7:15: "Yet if the unbelieving one leaves, let him leave; the brother or the sister is not under bondage in such cases, but God has called us to peace."

What does this mean? Should a woman submit to her unsaved husband? YES!!! But here's the kicker—such a woman will learn to become super discerning. She'll have to be led by him, but the only time she can resist his leadership is if he tries to encourage her to sin! That's because by doing so, he offends the higher authority, and man's authority can't override God's authority. Nevertheless, if he makes a simple-minded decision and the wife does not agree with his decision, she must submit to him if his decision is not offensive to God. If you want to keep Jezebel out of your heart and home, you'd better follow God's order because Jezebel is the principality of disorder!

Sound of Fire 439

Knowledge means you know better, but understanding means you'll do better.

Sound of Fire 440

Love answered before there even was a question.

Sound of Fire 441

Wisdom comes in through open doors (will) or through the storms that beat upon those doors (trials). Either way, if we ask for it, it's coming in. Open the door. It's easier that way.

Sound of Fire 442

Behind every Satanic plot is a bunch of demons who are determined to keep you from accessing whatever it is that they see in the spirit realm heading your way. It's up to you whether they succeed or not.

Sound of Fire 443

We are either problem-focused or solution-minded; either way, we can never complain about a problem until we can present a solution to that problem, or be the solution to that problem.

Sound of Fire 444
You are somebody's lesson.

Sound of Fire 445
You are already wealthy; you just have to tap in to the abundance that Christ allotted for you. Poverty and struggling is a result of you losing your faith and tapping out (looking for external means).

Sound of Fire 446
A believer who walks in holiness is like a bright light. A believer who loves the world is like a man with a hangover. Expose him to the light and he will curse you.

Sound of Fire 447
Dying to self is like being hungry and watching everyone around you eat takeout, while resisting the junk food because you want what's being prepared!

Sound of Fire 448
If everybody liked you, God wouldn't set a table for you because He wouldn't have anyone to honor you in front of. Enemies are essential to elevation!

Sound of Fire 449
Storms uncover motives. Those who have a true heart for

God will weather the storms and cry out to God for help, but those who have ungodly motives will manifest their true nature when a storm threatens to destroy whatever it is that they idolize (marriage, career, pride, money, etc.).

Sound of Fire 450

Trying to convince someone to like you is like auditioning to be a part of what God will ultimately have to deliver you from. Godly connections aren't forced, bought or manipulated.

Sound of Fire 451

God loves to hear us say, "I give up." That's because this means we've exhausted our own efforts and are now ready to give our burdens to the Lord.

Sound of Fire 452

Fasting is great because it tears down the flesh and uncovers the enemy's hiding places. It also puts you at the mercy of God ... powerless, desperate and broken. What God then sees is a powerless (submitted) believer and the enemy attacking him or her. This provokes God to move immediately on the believer's behalf and leaves the enemy with no place to hide and no legal grounds to be there.

Sound of Fire 453

A storm is nothing but the winds of change beating upon our comfort zones.

Sound of Fire 454
Push past yesterday. You're in a new day.

Sound of Fire 455
Conflict starts with self.

Sound of Fire 456
Freedom starts with God.

Sound of Fire 457
Some women refuse to let a man drive their cars, but will let a man test drive their bodies. This tells us that many women place more value in things than they place in themselves. It's no wonder then that their cars outlast their relationships.

Sound of Fire 458
People proudly say, "You reap what you sow" when they've been done wrong, but are quick to say, "Let him who is without sin cast the first stone" when they are the wrongdoers. When Joshua said, "Choose ye this day whom you will serve," he wasn't talking about which scriptures you want to serve. You can't be right all the time. Sometimes, you actually do have to repent.

Sound of Fire 459
If you chase prophecies while running from the Word, you can be rest assured that you're going to run into a witch or a warlock and think that person is a prophet.

Sound of Fire 460
Your plans for you aren't necessarily God's plans for you. Sometimes, a storm is just you going in one direction when God has called you to walk in another direction

Sound of Fire 461
Satan doesn't bind you; he doesn't have power to do that. You bind yourself! He just offers you the tools you need to do it by yourself.

Sound of Fire 462
Wet hands aren't necessarily clean hands. How many of us have been in a public restroom and seen someone come out of a stall, stick their hands under a faucet quickly (not applying soap), snatch a paper towel and barely wipe their hands before tossing it into the trash. They then grab the dirty door handle and proceed out of the bathroom dirtier than they were when they came in. If you look at their hands, they are still wet, so you may trust them to prepare your food, shake your hand or lovingly grab your child's face because you see the moisture on their hands. Nevertheless, their hands are a filthy gathering of germs, bacteria, dirt and maybe even a virus or two. The same goes for the church. Not everyone in church is trying to avoid sin. Many purposely pursue sin; and church, to them, is nothing more than running water to wash their sins away time and time again. But they aren't seeking God's heart; they don't desire to be pure, even though they go out of their way to appear to be pure. Understand that the body and the heart can be in two

separate zip codes. The body can be in the church while the heart is in the club! Let's seek to be free for real, saints. People who attempt to get over on God are only fooling themselves.

Sound of Fire 463
Sometimes, we're flattered when we should be offended and we are offended when we should be flattered. For this reason, we should stop, think and pray before deciding how we feel about certain things.

Sound of Fire 464
I was seriously about to ask the Lord to surround me with people who are like me ... people who have a heart like mine, but then He checked me before I could even get started on the prayer. If I was surrounded by people who were like me, I'd end up flattered, content, thankful and stuck! We need to be challenged because challenges give us something to overcome. It's our differences that provoke offense or growth. I choose to grow.

Sound of Fire 465
You will never gain understanding if you do not have knowledge. After all, how can you understand what you do not know?

Sound of Fire 466
Imagine this: Janice and Jessica are both in college, but Janice's classes in the first semester requires that she carry

more books than Jessica. Because of this, Jessica is always helping Janice with her books ... taking some of the burden upon herself and even going out of her way to carry Janice's books to her class before rushing off to her own. In the next semester, Jessica's classes give her more books, while Janice is required by her classes to carry far less than she had before. Nevertheless, when Janice realizes that Jessica's load is heavy, she begins to avoid her, even though she is friendly when she runs into her. Jessica manages to carry her load without any man's help and she becomes stronger, wiser and more disciplined, whereas Janice continues to surround herself with people who are willing to carry her loads, even though she is unwilling to carry theirs. Which one are you? Be honest with yourself. After all, how you are to others will and does affect you.

Sound of Fire 467
Sometimes, we apply for the right positions in the wrong places or with the wrong people.

Sound of Fire 468
Sometimes, we keep getting rejected because we keep applying for the wrong positions!

Sound of Fire 469
We can't expect God to answer questions we haven't yet asked!

Sound of Fire 470

Sometimes, we ask God questions that He has already answered. God does NOT change His mind. Accept His answer and move on.

Sound of Fire 471

Not too long ago, I had to take some medicine for heartburn. That's because I couldn't stomach what I took in. The same goes for what we allow in our hearts. Oftentimes, a storm is nothing but spiritual heartburn brought on by what we've allowed in our hearts.

Sound of Fire 472

If you've asked God for it and you've believed God for it, it was and is yours starting from the moment you believed. Oftentimes, the manifestation doesn't come immediately because you've asked but haven't yet believed.

Sound of Fire 473

As long as we trust God, we will obey Him. As long as we are obeying God, we are advancing towards the manifestations of what we've been praying for.

Sound of Fire 474

Unfamiliar roads make you slow down and pay attention to where you're going.

Sound of Fire 475

Your decisions are the fingerprints of your heart.

Sound of Fire 476

Love settled our debt. That's why you are to owe no man nothing but to love him

Sound of Fire 477

Your heart is your life's refrigerator. What you put in it is what you'll take from it.

Sound of Fire 478

Your name is only as important as the individual you represent. David fought Goliath in the name of the Lord. Elijah called down fire from Heaven in the name of the Lord. They were both successful because they didn't come in their own names; they came in the name of the Lord. That's why the enemy LOVES to attack the character and reputation of a saint. In truth, he is attacking that person's name because he is trying to get others to associate that person's name with his (Satan's) and not with the name of Jesus. This demonic strategy is not only effective in a lot of cases, but causes so many of us to miss God because of what "we heard." That's why it's important to ask God about the people whose names are being attacked; that way, you do not accept the enemy's report versus the truth. Don't fund Satan's attempts to rid the body of another laborer, because the harvest is plenty, but the laborers are few. We need all the help we can get! Instead, pray and watch God blow your mind! He will redeem that person's name by first validating him or her as His servant and then discrediting those who've taken up weapons against that person's name. It's all about faith ...

not works. If you take a walk and make it a faith walk, you won't have to go the long route towards a blessing; faith is the vehicle that will get you to where you want to be and beyond in far less time than a bunch of works!

Sound of Fire 479

You are vessels of the Word of God, and as such, you are bearers of His infinite wisdom. The Bible says that wisdom is too high for a fool. In other words, do not be unequally yoked with an unbeliever because though you lower yourself to have him or her, that person will never be able to reach or cover you.

Sound of Fire 480

When you don't release people from their sins against you, you end up bearing the weight of the offense and the weight of the person who offended you!

Sound of Fire 481

Spiritual burdens are not supposed to be carried by natural people. Turn it over to Jesus ... daily.

Sound of Fire 482

Notice that doctors sometimes have to get people to bend in order to straighten them out. The Word does the same.

Sound of Fire 483

Sometimes, our desires stem from our voids, and our storms stem from our necessity.

Sound of Fire 484

What you want and what you need are not necessarily the same.

Sound of Fire 485

God can take a problem you've been struggling with for years and fix it overnight! Stop trying to fix the problem and go build your faith!

Sound of Fire 486

Your surname is a part of your legacy! Make sure it's one your children will be glad to wear!

Sound of Fire 487

Abstinence is counted from the last time you had sex, but purity is counted from the last time you took charge of your thoughts. There are a lot of impure men and women abstaining from sex. The impure saint is driven by selfish motives, but the pure saint is driven by love. By the way, if you're fooling around with anyone, including yourself, you are NOT abstinent. You're simply avoiding "normal" sex, but you're still having sex!

Sound of Fire 488

Gratitude is not a feeling ... it is an action word that has to be expressed to be genuine. In other words, thanking God with your mouth is nothing if you don't express your gratitude with your life.

Sound of Fire 489

Are you leaving your mark on the next generation or are you leaving a stain on them? Your mark is your signature ... a model they'd want to follow, but a stain is an accident ... something people try hard to wash away.

Sound of Fire 490

You can't side with the world and expect Jesus to be on your side.

Sound of Fire 491

The lukewarm person will go to hell if they do not repent. However, there is no such thing as lukewarm fire. If you don't believe me, confront the eye on your stove when it's lit.

Sound of Fire 492

Lust is found in the smoker's section of eternity.

Sound of Fire 493

Romantic (Eros) love is neither lost nor spent ... sometimes, we just invest it in the wrong people.

Sound of Fire 494

You can't have split level faith. When your faith is whole, you are whole, but when your faith is unstable, you are unstable.

Sound of Fire 495

We are all somewhere we never dreamed we would be, but

somehow, we find a reason to complain about something. At the same time, not being completely happy with where you are, helps you to keep dreaming and therefore pursuing something.

Sound of Fire 496

Unforgiveness is debt. It is when an offended person thinks they are owed something by the person who's offended him or her. Jealousy is also debt. It is when a person feels entitled and therefore owed what another person has, is getting or is expecting to receive. Either way, trying to make another human being indebted to you is the same as disregarding the shed blood of Jesus. After all, your debt was forgiven. How dare you turn around and place debt on another human being as if the sins you've committed against God are less than the offenses someone else has committed against you! How dare you feel entitled to what does not belong to you! Yes, we are favored by God, but that doesn't mean we are better than our brethren. Let's stay submitted to the call and stop forging God's signature on our sinful ways.

Sound of Fire 497

Woman of God, you don't belong to yourself, so you can't give yourself away.

Sound of Fire 498

The sun lights up the world, but the Son of God is the light of the world.

Sound of Fire 499

A wife who refuses to submit to her husband has a demon that is commonly referred to as a spirit husband.

Sound of Fire 500

If Jesus Christ is Lord over your life, He has to be Lord over your decisions. You can't restrict Him to certain areas of your life and expect Him to accept the limitations you've placed on Him.

Chapter 6

Sound of Fire 501

Love is central; everything in life revolves around it and draws its life from it. It's similar to the workings of our hearts.

Sound of Fire 502

What we allow in our ear gates and eye gates determines if the gates of hell are able to prevail against us.

Sound of Fire 503

You can't defeat the devil with words. He has already been defeated by the Word. You just have to remind him of it.

Sound of Fire 504

We're no better than our brothers and sisters in the Lord; we're just in different places.

Sound of Fire 505

Just like you can sow a seed, you can also bury a seed. The attitude in which you give and the ground you sow it in will determine the condition of that seed.

Sound of Fire 506

A man's last name is valuable to him. When he gives it to you, he is giving you a receipt for your love. When he requires sex before marriage, he is saying that you aren't worth his last name. Stop acting like a junkie in an alley trying to convince a drug dealer that the diamond he has is real. If you know you're valuable, stay in position, and the man who can afford you will approach your Maker and he will be willing to pay the price for you to have his last name.

Sound of Fire 507

We intentionally refrain from crimes that will get us locked up in jail, but we rarely refrain from behaviors (sins) that get us locked up in bondage.

Sound of Fire 508

Much of what happens to us happens because of us (i.e. divorce, incarceration, etc.)

Sound of Fire 509

Demons cannot repent. That's why you have to repent before you can get free of them.

Sound of Fire 510

Joy and peace are two realities that cannot be taken from you (outside of tragedy of course). They have to be given away.

Sound of Fire 511

Sanctified means to be set apart. When a woman who God has set apart from the world, marries a worldly man, she basically reveals her identity, location and assignment to the enemy. He will utilize his access to her through her beau to destroy her, destroy her name, destroy her ministry and destroy her children. This is similar to an American soldier who's stationed in Afghanistan having tea with an Afghani woman in the center of town while wearing his uniform. You can't give the enemy the chance to take you out and expect him not to take it.

Sound of Fire 512

If you don't love yourself, you cannot and will not embrace the love that God has for you. Self-rejection always starts with a person rejecting what God says and feels about them, to embrace what others have said about them.

Sound of Fire 513

If there is anyone in your ear telling you that all men are cheaters, you need to correct that person and then take a safe distance from them. Sometimes, women ask God for husbands and get delayed because they have some woman in their circle who keeps vomiting on their hearts. Esther was massaged with perfumed oils for six months to detoxify her and give her a pleasant scent, but many women today have been massaged with lies for so long that they stink with unforgiveness. These same women can't seem to understand why "the king" refuses to see them.

Sound of Fire 514

Satan's favorite weapon to use against you is a person whose opinion you value the most.

Sound of Fire 515

We're just passing through life on our way to eternity. Make sure you're on the right path so you'll end up on the right side of eternity.

Sound of Fire 516
Humility is strength, but pride is the shadow of weakness.

Sound of Fire 517
There are some diseases that once you catch them, you become immune to them. A vaccination is nothing but low doses or dead strains of a disease designed to get your immune system to build up a defense against future infections from that particular disease. Guess what? As it is in the natural, so it is in the spirit! Some of the attacks we endure are designed to strengthen our faith so that we will be guarded from future darts by our new and improved shields of faith. Even though the storms rage up against you, please know that you are protected by the Most High God!

Sound of Fire 518
If you attack the enemy's camp when you're not under attack, you'll foil the enemy's plans to attack you.

Sound of Fire 519
A weak man's strength is in his arms. A strong man's strength is in his ability to put his arms together, lower himself to his knees and send up an effective prayer.

Sound of Fire 520
Stop trying to make blind folks see you! Anyone who can't see you isn't called to walk with you!

Sound of Fire 521

Sometimes, you just have to praise Him without the music so that when you press in, you'll press into His presence and not your emotions.

Sound of Fire 522

Yes, giants do fall, but the problem with many believers is that they always assume they are the Davids and everyone who contends with them is a Goliath. Listen up. Sometimes, believers fall because they keep doubling as a giant in someone else's life. Many think that because they use nice little Christian words and a few "hallelujahs" that they are automatically on the right side of a battle. How about this? Sometimes, you're in the wrong; sometimes, they are in the wrong. Then again, there are those times when both of you are wrong! Don't assume that you have God's backing. Pray and ask God for insight; that way, you don't end up being man-handled by someone you thought was smaller than you!

Sound of Fire 523

Remember that the Lord (in His earth suit) had no beauty or majesty that we should desire Him, but He was all God! What does this tell us? God often hides some of the most beautiful and anointed men and women of God behind average and not-so-appealing earth suits. He does this so that by seeing, we cannot see. Please understand that sin has blinded us to the things of the Spirit, therefore, we have to walk in the Spirit to see the hidden treasures of the

Kingdom! Stop looking for your God-appointed spouse through those scaly eyes of yours and get in the Spirit!

Sound of Fire 524
Don't confuse your love for a song or the thrill you get when you hear your favorite scripture, with your love for God. Love is too deep to ground itself in your emotions.

Sound of Fire 525
The more God uses you, the more the enemy will rise up against you. Nevertheless, his weapons are powerless against submitted believers who are clothed with the whole armor of God.

Sound of Fire 526
Growing up poor made us appreciate the bottom of the pot. You see, we didn't throw food away. We often found ourselves scraping the bottom of the pot to get what was left out of it. Nothing went to waste. That's what we ought to do as believers. Every test and trial is an experience that is potent enough to not only teach and benefit us, but is effective enough to teach and benefit others. This means that instead of complaining about the storms, we should always get as much wisdom out of each storm as possible. Sure, you may feel like you're at your lowest point, but that's not a bad thing. Just scrape the bottom of the storm until the wisdom you uncover causes the storm to give up her wealth.
In every storm, there is an opportunity to complain and worry; then again, there is an opportunity to get wisdom.

What you take from the storms will determine whether you throw away valuable knowledge (meaning you'll see that storm again), or if you'll get that knowledge and learn to become a storm chaser.

Sound of Fire 527

In every classroom, there are students who came to learn and students who came because they felt like they had no choice. If you know the difference between the two, you won't waste your time or oil on the unteachable.

Sound of Fire 528

You can't buy favor.

Sound of Fire 529

Do not complain about the weapons that were formed against you. Instead, rejoice in the fact that they did not and will never prosper.

Sound of Fire 530

Obedience and honor look the same, but they flow from different places. We obey God because we fear Him and believe Him, but we honor God's Word because we love and trust Him. A child who obeys you is good, but only a son or a daughter can properly honor you.

Sound of Fire 531

A God-fearing, God-submitted spouse is worth waiting, praying and pressing for.

Sound of Fire 532

Life is but a series of exchanges. You hand the person at the checkout money in exchange for the groceries in your cart. This changes things. You end up with less money but more groceries. Your job trains you and then, you give them your time in exchange for money. This changes things. You end up with less time but more money. Someone says something to you and you exchange words with them. This changes you. You end up considering their thoughts at the expense of your own beliefs. Understand this ... the word "exchange" is comprised of two words and they are "ex" and "change." The word "ex" means "former" and of course, the word "change" means to alter something or someone. When you communicate with people, you are exchanging your thoughts for theirs. If these people are "regulars" in your life, they WILL challenge your current beliefs and many of those beliefs may become your former beliefs. In other words, the people we associate with have the power to change our minds, which means they have the power to change our lives! After all, your life is nothing but an exchange. You express and live by your beliefs and in exchange, your mindset becomes your manifestation. Remember the Word! God said that a friend of wise men will grow wiser, but a friend of fools will be destroyed!

Sound of Fire 533

Stop trying to tell that man how valuable or anointed you are if he didn't have to pay the price for you!

Sound of Fire 534

God places His protection on His children, but Satan places security tags on his children. The mistake some women make is getting one of Satan's sons and taking him to church, hoping that God will cut Satan's tag off the man or stop the alarm that keeps going off in their spirit.

Sound of Fire 535

A diamond never walks up to a potential buyer and sparkles. It stays in place and sparkles from where it stands. Knowing the value of the diamond, the jeweler places a high price tag on it and locks it behind a case where people can see it, but can't easily steal it. Many people will look at the diamond and remark on its beauty, but those same people will pass it by. It's not because they don't want it; they pass it by because they can't afford it. That diamond can be on display for years, but the jeweler won't lower its price because he knows that eventually, someone will come along who can afford that diamond and is willing to pay the price for it! That same someone would have overlooked that diamond if it was priced too low because it would cause them to question the value of the diamond. The person who can afford it will take special care of that diamond because of the price they had to pay to purchase it! Don't be the diamond who comes from behind the case and ends up stolen by someone who does not know its value or appreciate its craftsmanship! If you stay put, someone will eventually come along who knows your value, can spiritually afford to cover you and has already paid the price for you!

Sound of Fire 536

When a customer is interested in purchasing a service from me, they reach out to me. As a matter of fact, I have a rule in business and that is ... I don't call customers; I let them call me. This includes people who email me, leave me their numbers and say, "Call me. I'm interested in ordering _____ service from you." Why is this? Because when a company calls a customer, that places the company at the mercy of the customer and the customer will (in 98 percent of the cases) attempt to set their own terms and prices, and that's never good! The customer will also try to make the company compete with another company by saying, "I talked with _____ company and they're willing to give me that service at this price. Could you offer me something better?" That's not entrepreneurship; that's back-alley bargaining! Why? When you do that, you are, in a sense, saying that what you are offering is not worth the price tag you've placed on it! Additionally, it causes the company to invest far more time in that particular customer than they would with the customers who've called them! Finally, when a company calls the customer, the customer will more than likely not purchase anything unless you're willing to bargain with them, so they will waste your time! When the customer calls the company, it's because the customer is willing to pay the price for the service without attempting to bargain or reason with the company. The customer recognizes the value of what he or she wants to purchase and is willing to pay the price and play by the rules! Listen up! Courtship is the same! When you reach out to a man and begin to pursue him, you place yourself at the mercy of that man. You are, in a sense, saying that you are not worth the price God has placed on your hand! Additionally, it causes you to invest far more time in an Ishmael than you would have if he'd pursued you. When a man pursues you, it's because he is willing to pay the price for your hand without attempting to discount you or get you to compete with other women! When a man pursues your hand, he is acknowledging the value of your hand and he won't waste your time!

Sound of Fire 537

Ladies, ladies, ladies ...
Be pursued!
Stop pursuing.
When you learn the value of who you are, you'll hide yourself.
Diamonds don't chase buyers.

Sound of Fire 538

A child's eyes are innocent. God's eyes are holy. Whatever you wouldn't subject a child to, you shouldn't subject God to.

Sound of Fire 539

Your life is a movie that the Lord is watching. Don't subject the Holy God to porn, profanity, gossip, slander, or anything that would make Him cast your movie in the fire.

Sound of Fire 540

It is possible to pursue the right thing in the wrong mindset.

Sound of Fire 541
Rejection should not be internalized, even when you experience it externally.

Sound of Fire 542
Life isn't always what you make it. Sometimes, it's what it makes you.

Sound of Fire 543
You will always gravitate towards what's already on the inside of you.

Sound of Fire 544
It is possible to have a wife and still not have a help meet.

Sound of Fire 545
It is possible to have a husband and still not have a covering.

Sound of Fire 546
It is possible to marry the wrong man while practicing abstinence. How so? Some women use abstinence as a tool of manipulation. Manipulation is witchcraft. When you use a godly tool in the wrong way, you will always catch the wrong men with it.

Sound of Fire 547
It is possible to abstain from sex and still not be abstinent.

Sound of Fire 548

Be careful that you don't get comfortable in the wrong mindset. It is normal for us, as humans, to look for stability, but sometimes, we become stable in instability. This means that we embrace wrongful mindsets and get comfortable in, with and because of those mindsets. I've learned that life, for us, is nothing short of a flight and while on this flight, we all choose various paths to get us to where we're assigned to be or where we're trying to be. During this journey, we get hurt, offended, embarrassed, persecuted, ridiculed, betrayed, abandoned, taken advantage of, taken for granted, rejected, etc. Our response to every negative thing will determine the paths we take and ultimately determine where we put on lives on autopilot. The truth is that many people took to the skies of life, found themselves in dysfunction and decided to level off there. They've grown accustomed to the turbulence of dysfunction and they've allowed their pain to become their realities. Because of this, they have stabilized themselves in instability and they've grown comfortable there! Understand this. We all go through, but it doesn't mean that we're supposed to accept defeat or delay. Sometimes, it means that we're flying at the wrong altitudes with the wrong attitudes—or sometimes, it means that we've gotten off course. At other times, interference is nothing but the enemy trying to redirect our paths! Either way, we have to take to the skies of life and press our way all the way through until we see God's glory, and from there, we navigate from glory to glory! Stop accepting instability; it is NOT your portion! God has called you to fly above everything that is opposing you; that way, you don't become comfortable in what was supposed to be beneath you! That way, you don't become what you're going through!

Sound of Fire 549

It is possible to memorize scriptures and not know the Word.

Sound of Fire 550

Some people hang out with and tell all of their secrets to the weapons that were formed against them.

Sound of Fire 551

When you repeatedly attack the enemy's camp, you become a thorn in his side.

Sound of Fire 552

Credit cards and impatience go hand in hand.

Sound of Fire 553

When narcissists get married, they marry themselves vicariously through their spouses.

Sound of Fire 554

It is possible to be single and content.

Sound of Fire 555

It is possible to be married and lonely.

Sound of Fire 556

It is possible to be soul tied and abstinent.

Sound of Fire 557

Unforgiveness is a soul tie between you and the person you're mad at.

Sound of Fire 558

There are some people who stay bound simply because they think they need certain demons (pride, offense, unforgiveness, pornea, seduction, etc.).

Sound of Fire 559

Impatience doesn't make God move faster. It only delays or prohibits people from getting whatever it is that they are praying for simply because they are in the wrong spirit.

Sound of Fire 560

God's love is still even when you're all over the place.

Sound of Fire 561

Let them talk. They can't change God's mind about you.

Sound of Fire 562

Prayer changes things; faith changes people.

Sound of Fire 563

Love wins souls and changes hearts.

Sound of Fire 564
When you don't respond to foolishness, you give God the green light to respond.

Sound of Fire 565
What you thought you lost was nothing but a setup for God to show up and get the glory!

Sound of Fire 566
Some people have embraced the name of God, but not the heart of God. That's why the enemy keeps spanking them over an open fire.
(Example: Sons of Sceva.)

Sound of Fire 567
Slang is word rebellion.

Sound of Fire 568
Whatever you announce, you give life to! That's why you have to renounce some things in order to terminate them!

Sound of Fire 569
A relative isn't always someone you're related to by blood; it's whomever you can relate to. With that being said, stop looking at the family tree that you were born into and start paying attention to the tree that you yourself have created! That speaks volumes about you!

Sound of Fire 570

Every person is a "formation" of whatever it is that he or she is submitted to. God formed mankind, but sin deformed us. That's why we have to be transformed by the renewing of our minds.

With that being said, when you attempt to romantically link yourself with someone who has not yet been transformed by God, you are admitting that your transformation is not yet complete.

Sound of Fire 571

A woman sits on the couch and talks to the man God did not approve for her life. She attempts to reason with him; she attempts to express her love to him and she attempts to convince him to put his guards down. What she does not know is that he has to hear from God before he is able to hear from her.

Sound of Fire 572

All warfare is not internal; sometimes, it's external. If you know where the warfare is coming from, you'll know where to point your weapon (Sword).

Sound of Fire 573

The prefix "div" is a mathematical term which means to separate, to deviate, to break apart and to differ. It is where the words divorce and divide comes from. It also means a stupid or foolish person. Hear this: The reason the church is so divided today is because we've gotten so caught up with numbers that we have started placing our faith in numbers. Be reminded of what happened to Israel when David commanded Joab to count the Israelites. Because David was acting like a foolish person and he was ready to put his faith in numbers, 70,000 Israelites died. That's a lot of blood for one leader to have on his hands! Anytime you try to mix numbers with the Kingdom, you will cause a great falling away and end up with a lot of blood on your hands! You have to trust God and let Him order your steps; that way, you don't try to blaze your own trail. Any leader who is led astray by selfish ambition has or will have a lot of blood on his or her hands because that leader will immediately subject himself or herself to the law of numbers! Also, please note that when "div" comes in, it releases spirits of divorce, deviation (rebellion), division AND divination! Stop counting people and money and just know that you can count on God.

Sound of Fire 574
If you haven't yet embraced God's perfect love, you are not yet ready to receive love from an imperfect man or woman.

Sound of Fire 575
Religiousness is a sound proof room that keeps many from hearing God.

Sound of Fire 576
Worship without love is just noise in the ears of God.

Sound of Fire 577

Blessed is the man who puts away self to receive the One who is greater than he is.

Sound of Fire 578

Worship isn't just a compilation of words; it's full surrender.

Sound of Fire 579

Authentic worship positions you to receive whatever it is that you've been praying for.

Sound of Fire 580

There's no such thing as partial surrender with God. It's all or nothing with Him.

Sound of Fire 581

Your time is one of the most valuable assets that you have. That's why it makes the perfect seed. Understand this—whatever you sow, you will receive an increase of. When you spend time with God, He increases your time. When you spend time praising God, He will give you more reasons to praise Him.

Sound of Fire 582

You're supposed to behold the Lamb of God, but some of y'all be holding candy-coated baby devils. Then you bring that demon under the anointing and you wonder why Satan runs in, snatches his child from you, loads Satan Jr. or Satania up in his or her religious car seat and drives away.

Sound of Fire 583

People often marry one another's potential but divorce each other's reality.

Sound of Fire 584

Stop trying to tell that man how valuable or anointed you are if he didn't have to pay the price for you!

www.ingramcontent.com/pod-product-compliance
Lightning Source LLC
Chambersburg PA
CBHW061721020426
42331CB00006B/1035